BEGINNING GUITAR FOR THE SONGWRITER

Guitar Accompaniment for Composition

Ian Robbins

©2019 Ian Robbins

All rights reserved. No part of this book may be reprinted or reproduced or utilized in any form or by any electronic, mechanical, or other means, now known or hereafter therein, including photocopying and recording, or in any information storage or retrieval system, without permission in writing from the publisher.

Trademark notice: Product or corporate names may be trademarks or registered trademarks, and are used only for identification and explanation without intent to infringe.

Library of Congress Cataloging-in-Publication Data
Name: Robbins, Ian Matthew, author.
Title: Beginning Guitar for the Songwriter/ Ian Robbins
Identifiers: LCCN 7105685391| ISBN 9781732996809 (paperback) | ISBN 9781732996816

ISBN: 9781732996809 (paperback)
ISBN: 9781732996816 (ebook)

Dedicated to my wife, my parents, and Dr. Rachel Yoon.
Your unwavering support allows me to accomplish everything I do ❤️.

Table of Contents

Foreward 1

Introduction: The Basic Fundamentals 2

  Acoustic Guitars 2

  Electric Guitars 5

  Guitar Terminology 12

    Strings 12

    Frets 14

    Neck 15

    Headstock 16

    Bridge 18

    Soundhole 20

    Pick-ups 20

    Volume Knobs 23

    Tone Knobs 24

    Pick-up Selector Switch 24

  Other Features 25

    Amplifiers 27

Chapter 1: Guitar Technique Basics 30

  Right Hand Position 32

  Left Hand Position 38

  Tuning 42

    Electronic Tuners: 42

    Tuning by Ear: 44

  Guitar Nomenclature 46

    Staff Notation 46

    Tablature 46

    Chord Diagrams 48

  Em: 49

  Am: 50

  C: 52

  G: 53

  D: 54

  Chapter 1 Practice Progressions: 56

Chapter 2: Open Chords and Strum Patterns 57

  Rests 59

  E: 60

  E7: 61

  A: 62

- A7: 63
- Dm: 64
- G7: 65
- D7: 66
- **Chapter 2 Practice Progressions:** 67

Chapter 3: More Open Chords and Syncopated Strum Patterns 68

- **Counting 16th Note Rhythms** 69
  - Picking Directions for 16th Note Rhythmic Groupings 69
- B7: 72
- C7: 73
- Asus2: 74
- Dsus2: 75
- Cadd9: 76
- **Chapter 3 Practice Progressions:** 77

Chapter 4: Progression Creation, Transposition and Arpeggiation 78

- **The Capo** 82
  - Placing the Capo 82
- **Interpreting Progressions as Roman Numerals** 86
- **Arpeggiation** 87
- **Chapter 4 Practice Progression Creation:** 90

Chapter 5: Meter, Triplets and Alternating Bass 92

- Time Signatures 92
- Dotted notes 93
- Meter 95
- 6/8 Time 95
- Triplets 97
- Asus4: 99
- Dsus4: 100
- Esus4: 101
- Alternating Bass Note Accompaniment 102
- **Chapter 5 Practice Progressions:** 104

Chapter 6: Introduction to Barre Chords and Fingerstyle 105

- Barring 105
- F (basic): 107

- Dm7 108
- Movable Chord Shapes 109
- Pick playing vs. Fingerstyle 109
- The Right Hand 110
- Right Hand Technique 111
  - The Follow-through 115
- Chapter 6 Practice Progressions: 120

Chapter 7: Barre Chords and Fingerstyle Continued 121
- F (Four Strings): 121
- Bb (four strings) 122
  - The Movable Bb Chord 123
- Individual vs. Simultaneous Fingerstyle Attack 124
  - Creating Right Hand Patterns 125
- Chapter 7 Practice Progressions: 128

Chapter 8: Full Barre Chords and Power Chords 129
- F: 130
- Bb: 131
  - Transitioning from the 6th string to 5th string Barre Chord 132
- Modifiable Barre Chords 133
- Fm: 134
- F7: 135
- Bbm: 136
- Bb7: 137
- Power (5) Chords: 138
- E5: 138
- A5: 139
- Movable Power (5) Chords 140
- F5: 140
- Bb5: 141
- Chapter 8 Practice Progressions: 143

Chapter 9: Roots on the 6th String and Palm Muting 144
- Natural Note Names on the 6th String 144
- Memorizing Note Names 145
  - Note Names on the 6th String 145
- Cycle of 4^{ths} and Circle of 5^{ths} 146

  Transposing Barre Chords 147

 Palm Muting Technique 149

 Chapter 9 Practice Progressions: 152

Chapter 10: Roots on the 5th String and Offbeat Rhythms 153

 Natural Note Names on the 5th String 153

  Note Names on the 5th String 154

  Moveable Barre Chords with the 5th String Root 154

 Learning to Combine the 6th and 5th string Moveable chords 155

  Note Names on the 6th and 5th String 155

 Executing Off Beat Rhythms 159

Conclusion: Now What? 160

About the Author 161

Foreward:

Who are you? You are a creator, imaginative and unique. You construct music and lyrics, melodies and harmonies. Groove flows through you, your surroundings inspire you. You live to compose, and you compose how you live. You are the modern songwriter; perhaps a singer 🎤, perhaps a keyboardist 🎹 and maybe both. Maybe you are just getting started on your musical journey and have not yet chosen an instrument. If any of these are the case, you are lacking a fundamental tool 🔧 in your songwriter's toolbox: an understanding of the guitar 🎸.

Why is the guitar so important if you can already compose on the piano? The answer to this is the most obvious thing of all. It is because the guitar is a different instrument. This means a completely separate structure of how notes are arranged. The tuning of a guitar means that a chord voicing that would be extremely simple on the piano turns into an arthritis inducing stretch when transferred to the guitar. A chord on the piano which would require elastic fingers to achieve the desired stretches potentially turns into a fairly convenient fingering on the guitar fretboard. There is also a difference in how each respective instrument executes accompaniment rhythms. A guitar can produce rhythms due to the fact that you can strum both downwards and upwards in succession. While the piano maintains an advantage in terms of having more fingers (and therefore pitches) available for chord construction, it is on the verge of impossible to strum a piano (and have it sound musical). The guitar maintains timbres, characteristics of musical sound, that are difficult to recreate on even the best of synthesizers and note sustain potential that would function differently than a piano's sustain pedal. As the piano by definition is a percussion instrument, the guitar tends also to function as a rhythmic tool, achieving percussive effects by string muting (or even playing the body of an acoustic like a hand drum).

As you can see, by adding another compositional instrument to your arsenal you will be adding large amounts of potential ideas to your songs. A great way to solve writer's block is by simply picking up a different instrument (and on the guitar you can even experiment with different tunings) and letting the music come to you due to the nature of that instrument's layout.

I hope this book allows for you to unleash a cavalcade of musical creativity you may not have achieved previously. Lastly, the initial steps of learning this instrument may seem tedious and frustrating. Remember to be patient with yourself and rely on daily repetition. The more often you get your hands on the instrument, the faster your development will be.

Introduction: The Basic Fundamentals

As you may know, there are two categories of guitar: **Electric** and **Acoustic**

The acoustic guitar breaks down into the following categories: **Steel String** and **Nylon String**

Allow me to explain both of these instrument types and how they would benefit or hinder the development of a songwriter who is first learning the instrument, and what types of styles these instruments are generally used for.

Acoustic Guitars

String Type: Nylon

Nylon String Guitar

Pros while learning: Softer strings will be less painful on the fingers, wider string spacing will allow chords to be formed without accidental contact with on fingers on different strings.

Cons while learning: Wider spacing of strings can make for difficult stretches for those with smaller fingers, often quieter in volume than a steel string instrument, much harder to change strings on a traditional instrument.

Pros when skills are developed: Unique tone, wider string spacing much more ideal for fingerstyle technique.

Cons when skills are developed: Not the ideal guitar type to strum with a pick.

Musical styles: Classical, Flamenco, Latin, R&B.

String Type: Steel

Steel String Guitar

Pros while learning: Larger body leads to louder natural volume, closer string spacing allows for less strenuous finger stretching.

Cons while learning: Steel strings tend to be a heavier gauge which makes them harder to press down, higher strings will be the most painful of all guitar types to use before calluses are developed, The bigger body size on most steel string acoustics can be hard to reach around for smaller individuals.

Pros when skills are developed: Familiar tone, great for strumming or fingerstyle, "electric" guitar techniques more available on this instrument as compared to a nylon string guitar.

Cons when skills are developed: Barre chord shapes can be a bit fatiguing even when strength is developed.

Musical styles: Pop, Folk, Country, Rock.

Electric Guitars

There are numerous amounts of brands and models of electric guitars. It would take an entire book to catalog every type of electric guitar available on the market today. The ones I have listed are the most commonly found amongst songwriters and beginners. None are better or worse than the other, just different. Chose a guitar based on tone when you begin. Decide what you prefer by asking a more experienced player to play for you. Your fingers will grow accustomed to which ever neck scale and shape you choose. Eventually you will want to own multiple types of guitars to take advantage of the different features provided to you by each instrument. Below you will find the most regularly purchased guitar types:

Guitar Type: Stratocaster

Stratocaster with Maple Neck

Neck Wood: Maple (brighter tone) or Rosewood* (darker tone).

Body Shape: Dual cutaway solid body.

Pickups: Three single coil pick-ups.

Pros while learning: Easy access to all frets, relatively lightweight.

Cons while learning: Depending on the set up, may go out of tune if a string breaks, single coils may be noisy on less expensive instruments.

Pros when skills are developed: Great for bluesy or rhythmic playing, 5 way pick-up selection allows for a wide range of tones, tremolo bar can be used.

Cons when skills are developed: Depending on the set up the tremolo system may be hard to quickly change to alternate tunings.

Musical styles: Funk, Blues, Rock, Surf, R&B, Soul, Neo-soul.

Guitar Type: Telecaster

Telecaster

Neck Wood: Maple (brighter tone).

Body Type: Single cutaway solid body (or semi hollow body).

Pickups: Two Single Coil pick-ups.

Pros while learning: Simple pick-up configuration, fairly simple to restring.

Cons while learning: Thicker neck profile may be difficult for players with smaller fingers, bright tone is a bit unforgiving.

Pros when skills are developed: Telecasters are great at enhancing nuance within one's playing, very distinct tone.

Cons when skills are developed: No tremolo system, not as easy to access higher frets as with a dual cutaway.

Musical styles: Country, Rock, R&B.

Guitar Type: Les Paul

Les Paul

Neck Wood: Rosewood* (darker tone).

Body Type: Single cutaway solid body.

Pickups: Two Humbucker pick-ups.

Pros while learning: Scale length makes stretches feel a bit closer and string bend easier, humbucker pick-ups are less noisy than single coils.

Cons while learning: One of the heaviest solid body guitars on the market.

Pros when skills are developed: Quintessential rock n roll tone.

Cons when skills are developed: No tremolo system, limited tonal options.

Musical styles: Rock (all varieties)

Body Type: 335

336 (smaller body than a 335, same shape)

Neck Wood: Maple (brighter tone) or Rosewood* (darker tone).

Body Type: Double cutaway semi hollow.

Pickups: Two Humbucker pick-ups.

Pros while learning: Semi-hollow body provides a more acoustic resonance and fuller tone, scale length similar to a Les Paul.

Cons while learning: Large body may be hard to reach around for players with smaller arms, also could be hard to sit with for long periods of time.

Pros when skills are developed: Extremely versatile instrument.

Cons when skills are developed: Would not be able to use as much gain as a solid body (without feeding back), no tremolo system.

Musical styles: Blues, Funk, Jazz, Rock, Fusion, R&B, Soul, Neo-soul.

Body Type: Super Strat

Ibanez Prestige

Neck Wood: Maple (brighter tone) or Rosewood* (darker tone).

Body Type: Dual cutaway solid body.

Pickups: Humbucker-Single coil-Humbucker (HSH).

Pros while learning: Tend to be among the lighter of the instruments, versatile tonal options.

Cons while learning: Certain neck profiles are quite different than other guitars (making it difficult to transfer to another instrument).

Pros when skills are developed: Often will have 24 frets (as opposed to the usual 21 or 22), easy to play fast leads, tremolo systems are very controllable and stay in tune under extreme circumstances.

Cons when skills are developed: Not always good for rhythm playing, certain tremolo systems will go completely out of tune if a string breaks.

Musical styles: Rock, Metal, Fusion.

*The use of Rosewood has been banned in many countries due to scarcity. Many guitar manufactures now use alternative dark sounding woods.

Guitar Terminology

It is important to understand the names of the parts of the instrument in order to proceed with learning how to play.

Strings

Guitars are traditionally strung with six strings, although it is quite common to see seven or more strings on modern instruments. I suggest learning on a six-string guitar to simplify the process. The strings in standard tuning will all be tuned to a different pitch. The thicker the string, the lower the pitch as they will be tuned less taut than the thinner strings. The lowest (thickest strings) will tend to be wound (coils) and the highest strings are known as "plain".

Have you ever placed a rubber band between your thumb and forefinger and plucked it to hear the sound? You probably noticed that the tighter you stretched the rubber band, the higher the pitch became. The guitar strings work off the same physical principle.

From lowest to highest string, a guitar is tuned E-A-D-G-B-E

Guitar strings

We refer to the lowest pitched E string as the 6th string and the highest pitched E string as the 1st string. This concept may seem counterintuitive at first as you look down at the guitar as it sits on your lap. Remember we are counting up from the ground and not down from your vantage point. You may remember I mentioned some guitars are built with more than six strings. But it is almost physically impossible to add higher stings to a regular length guitar as the string tension would be so great it would snap the string before reaching pitch. So that way the HIGHEST string on any guitar would be the 1st string, therefore achieving a unifying numbering system across all guitar types. This also helps to unify string labeling across all families of fretted instruments such as bass guitar, ukulele, banjo, mandolin, etc. It is very important to memorize the strings by name as well as by number.

E(6)-A(5)-D(4)-G(3)-B(2)-E(1)

Frets

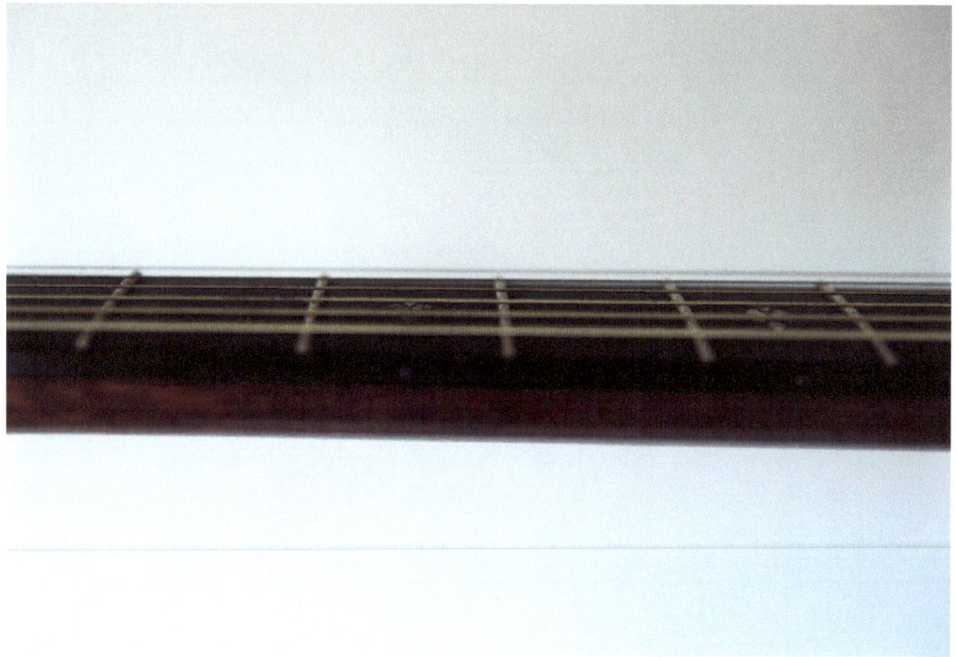

Guitar Frets

The frets are the metal bars laying horizontally across the neck. The frets serve as the stopping point for each string, thereby shortening the "sounding" length. By shortening a string, the string produces a higher pitch. The higher up you fret a note on a given string, the higher in pitch the sound becomes. The frets are arranged to stop the string in a series of half steps (semitones). We count the first metal fret as the 1st fret. Along the side of most guitars you will see a collection of dots. These dots, or **fret markers**, serve as a guide to help you locate proper frets as you move up the neck (some classical nylon string guitars do not have any fret markers). The single dots represent odd numbered frets, often beginning on the third fret (although some acoustics do not have markers until the 5th fret). Almost every guitar will have a double dot located at the 12th fret. The 12th fret is significant in that the string fretted from that point would sound an octave higher than the unfretted, or **open**, string. At that point the layout of dots will repeat itself with the first dot located on the 15th fret (representative of being an octave higher than the third fret).

Neck

Guitar Neck

The **neck** 🦒 of the guitar extends from the body and is where the hand presses down on the strings to produce different pitches. The front of the neck is known as the **fretboard.** Guitars have either bolt-on necks (which will be apparent by screws connecting the neck to the body of the guitar) or solid necks (no screws). A solid neck will generally allow for more sustain, but harder to fix if broken. A bolt-on neck can be replaced easily. Necks can be made of numerous wood types such as mahogany or maple. Some fretboards may be made from a different wood than the necks they sit atop of.

Headstock

The **headstock** sits atop the neck. It contains two crucial parts of the guitar's mechanics, the **nut** and the **tuning pegs.**

Nut

Guitar Nut

The nut can be made from a variety of materials but will most commonly be bone (or a bone substitute). It plays a role in stopping the string and therefore defining one "end". The string sounds at its longest point down at the nut and will produce its lowest pitch. The nut contains grooves for each one of the guitar strings so they may vibrate without moving position. Some electric guitars have a mechanism known as a **string tree** 🌳 that the higher strings pass through on the way to the tuning pegs.

Tuning Pegs

Tuning Pegs: 3 to a side

Tuning Pegs: 6 to a side

The tuning pegs serve the purpose of shortening or lengthening the strings of the guitar. The tuning pegs tighten or loosen each string thereby raising or lowering the pitch. You can trace each string from the nut to the tuning pegs in order to see which string will be affected by a given peg. Tuning pegs typically sit six to one side or three and three on each side.

If the tuning pegs sit six to a side than you will be able to tighten the strings by turning away from yourself (or counter clockwise). If the strings sit three to a side than the 6th, 5th and 4th strings will be tightened by turning away from yourself (counterclockwise), and the 3rd, 2nd and 1st strings are tightened by turned towards yourself (clockwise).

Tuning the tuning pegs even the slightest amount can vary the pitch of a string by quite a large amount. Be careful not to over tighten your strings as too much tension may cause them to break. If you find yourself turning the tuning peg a complete rotation, double check to make sure you are either a) turning the right peg for the given string you want to tune or b) not tuning the string to the wrong pitch.

Bridge

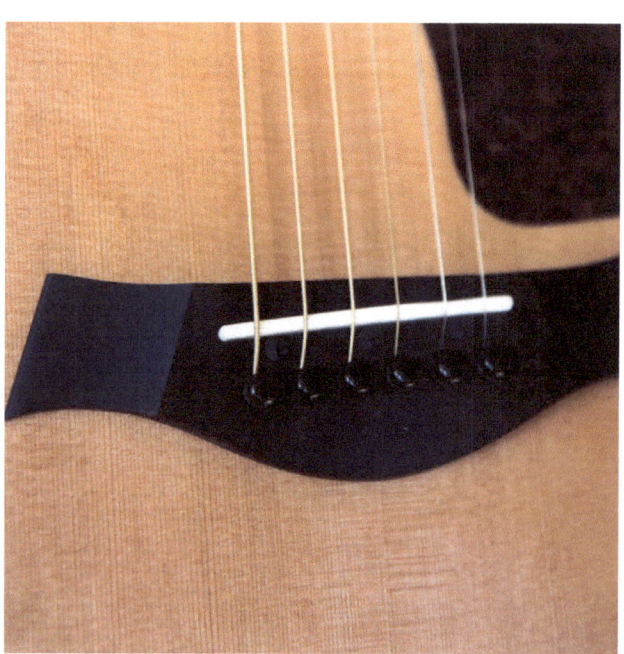

Acoustic Bridge

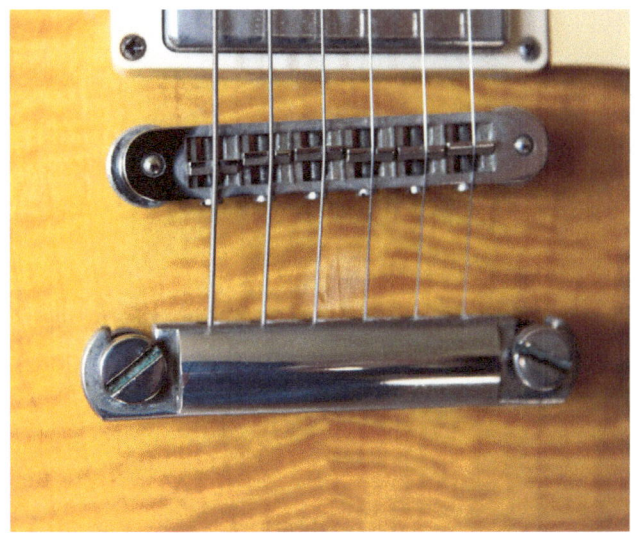
Electric Bridge: Les Paul

Electric Bridge: Telecaster

At the opposite end of the string from the nut you will find the **bridge**. The bridge will end the string similar to the nut, but other than very specific tremolo and tuning systems, you will not be able to manipulate the pitch of the string past the bridge without special tools. Most acoustic guitars have fixed bridges than cannot be adjusted easily, whereas the majority of electric guitars have individual **saddles** for each string. These devices allow for the guitar's intonation to be adjusted. It is advisable to not try to tamper with the saddles while you are still learning the instrument. Allow a professional guitar tech to set your intonation for you.

Acoustic bridges tend to be made of bone while electric bridges are made from metal.

Soundhole

Soundhole

Acoustic guitars and semi-hollow and hollow body electrics have holes in the body to help amplify the natural volume of the wood. Guitars with **soundholes** are in danger of feeding back if played through amplifiers at high volumes or with a lot of bass end coming from the amp.

Pick-ups

Electric and electric acoustic guitars must have pick-ups in order to transmit sound to an amplifier. The pick-up functions similar to a microphone, or even an ear 💡. It "hears" the sound the strings make and turns it into a signal that can be sent through a cable to an amplifier. Acoustic guitars often have pick-ups built into the bridge. You can also but acoustic guitar pick-ups that attach to the body or inside the sound hole. It is helpful to have a pick-up on your acoustic guitar if you plan to perform with other instrumentalists as even the loudest projecting guitar would have difficulty being heard over even a quiet drumset.

As mentioned earlier in the section on guitar types, electric guitars have 2 common pick-up types: **Single Coil**, and **Humbucker**.

Single Coil Pick-ups

Humbucker Pick-ups

Single coil pick-ups have a softer output (not necessarily a bad thing) than humbuckers. They tend to be a brighter sounding pick-up which can be used together in sequence to create a very distinct sound not attainable through humbuckers. The humbucker pick-ups provide a warmer and fuller sound which can be helpful in some ways but also difficult for beginners (remember any mistakes or extraneous string noise will be louder as well). Ideally you would chose pick-ups for the sake of their tone beyond any other factors and your ear should be able to detect what types of pick-ups are being used on different recordings.

Volume Knobs

Volume Knob

Any guitar with pick-ups should contain controls that allow you to manage the volume of each pick-up. They are not always labeled "volume", but will usually be the knob or knobs closest to the neck. Some guitars have separate volume knobs for individual pick-ups while others control two or more pick-ups simultaneously. Turning the knobs clockwise will increase the volume.

Tone Knobs

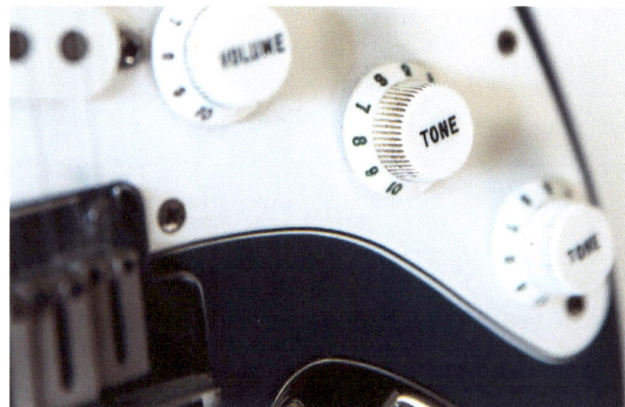
Tone Knobs

Similar to volume knobs in operation and placement, the **tone knobs** make each pick up either brighter or darker sounding. Turning the knobs clockwise will increase the brightness. Typically, each pick-up will have a separate tone control.

Pick-up Selector Switch

Selector Switch

The **selector switch** will allow you to choose which pick-up or pick-ups you want to activate. The amount of catches in the switch depends on the amount of pick-up combinations your guitar offers (standard is 3-5). If you have your pick-up selector facing upwards, you will select the "neck" pick-up (closest to the neck) which will be your darkest sound. Setting the pick-up selector all the way down will indicate the bridge pick-up is active and provide your brightest tone. Experiment strumming the strings as you go from one pick-up selection to the next examining the differences in tone.

Other Features

Tremolo Bar: Often screws into the bridge and will cause the bridge to move, thus dropping or raising the pitch of the strings. Only available on certain bridge types.

Tremolo Bar

Strap Buttons: One near the neck and one at the end of the body allows for you to attach a strap.

Strap button

Input Jack: This is where you plug in a 1/4 inch cable.

Input Jack

Amplifiers

A true in-depth description of amplifiers and all their features are beyond the scope of this text. Some key things to know about amps is that there are two prominent types available on the market today: Tube and Solid State.

Tube Amps: Contain transistor tubes which tend to sound warmer, especially on the overdrive setting.

Tube Amp Top

Solid State Amps: Digital simulations of tube sound. Usually containing more built-in effects and technologies.

Solid State Amp Top

Amplifier Parameters

All amps have different features included. The parameters listen below are the most commonly found across all types/brands of amps.

Volume Knob: Increases or decreases overall loudness.

Gain Knob: Pushes the amp so that a clean signal "breaks-up" or becomes saturated or distorted. This is known as overdrive.

Master Knob: Overall volume control which allows you to set the gain high (thus breaking up the sound) and the volume output lower.

Tone Knobs: Treble, Mid range, and Bass frequencies tend to all have adjustable controls.

Reverb: A type of echo-effect (not available on all amps).

Input Jack: The area to plug in your ¼ inch cable.

Amps may have numerous other features which should be explained in their individual user's guides. The basic information listed above should be enough to get you started.

Chapter 1: Guitar Technique Basics

Now that you understand basic technical guitar terminology, it's time to learn how to play!

Let us begin with a description of how to hold the instrument. Hold the guitar so that the thickest string is closest to the sky. The body of the guitar has a rounded curve. Rest the guitar on your right thigh in this area. Make sure the guitar body balances itself and you can sit without the guitar neck falling. The neck should aim upwards at a slight angle. Do not let the neck fall as you will have awkward hand angles when it comes time to place your hand on the instrument. You may also use a strap to hold the guitar at a comfortable angle.

How to sit with guitar: Angle 1

How to sit with guitar: Angle 2

The guitar is difficult to learn at first because it requires a lot of coordination between the right and left hands*.

*This book will assume you are planning to play with a right-handed guitar. Many left-handed people learn this way as well. Left handed guitars are very rare and more expensive. As both hands are equally important, there is not much of a benefit to owning a left-handed guitar unless you already learned on one. If you do want to learn left handed, no problem! Just reverse everything in this text to match your guitar's layout.

Right Hand Position

The right hand is called the picking hand. It is how the attack of the sound is produced. The right hand can strike the strings in several ways; with each individual finger (known as finger picking) or with a device called a pick.

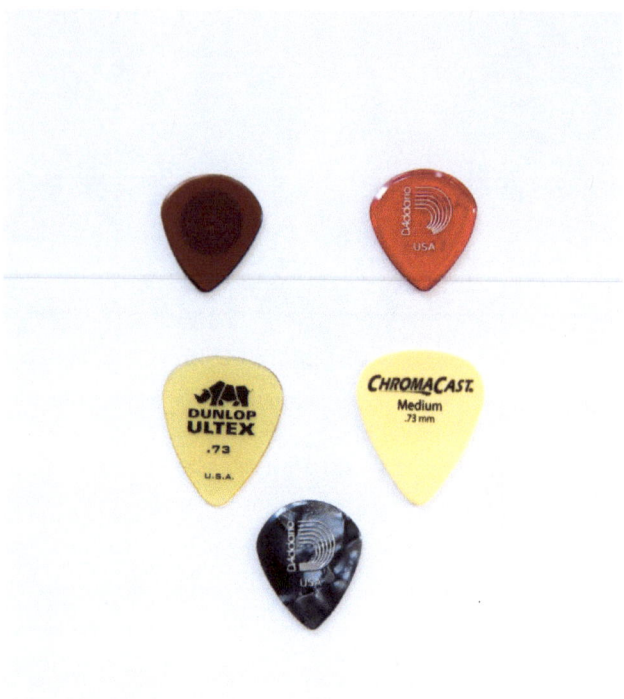

Picks

We will begin to play using pick strumming technique. Finger picking will be covered in the later portion of this book.

To learn how to properly grasp the pick, first make a soft fist with you left hand, leaving the thumb outstretched.

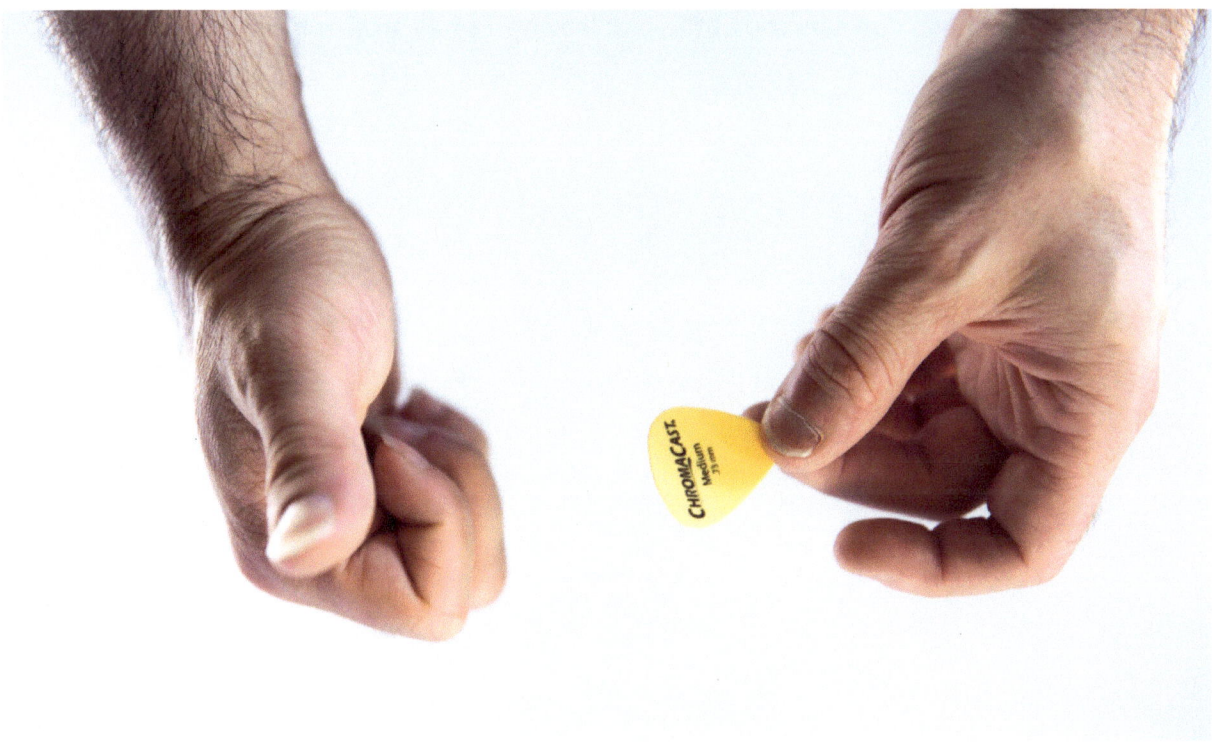

Fist with thumb outstretched

Next place the pick onto your hand so that the pointed end faces directly away from the flat surface of the nail on your index finger.

Fist with thumb out pick placement

Lastly, close your thumb down on top of the pick leaving a small area of the pick exposed.

Pick in hand: Correct

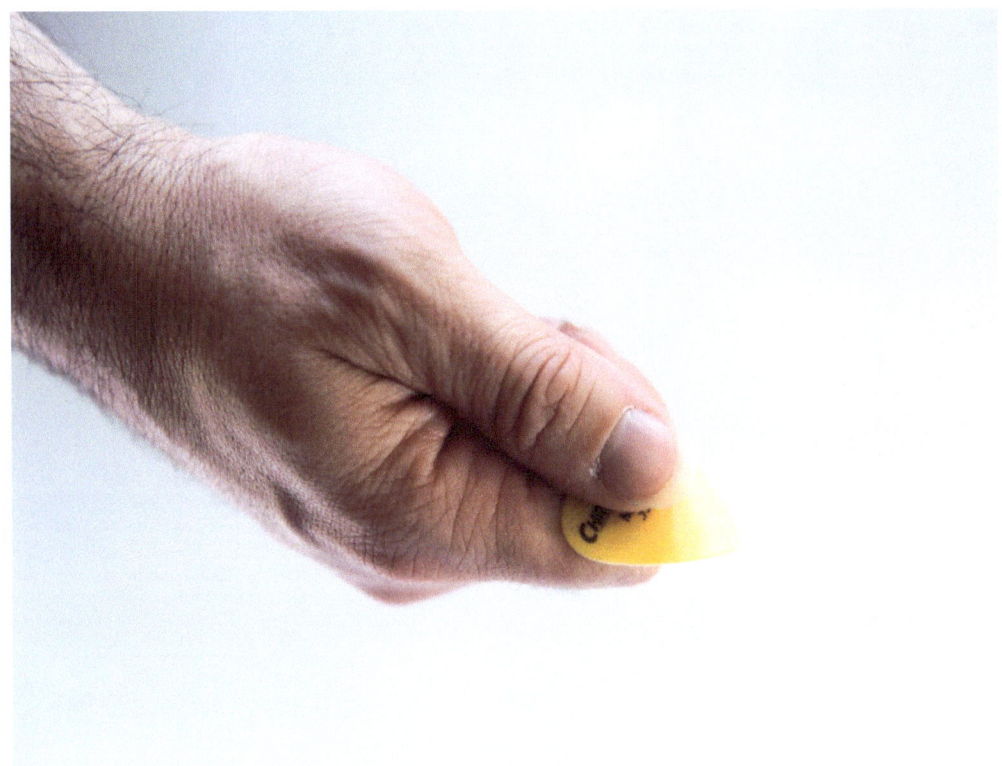

Pick in hand: **INCORRECT**
Please stop that at once.

Grip the pick firmly so that if you flick it with your left hand, the pick does not move. Remember when we pick the strings, the strings are barriers that by nature will try to dislodge the pick from your grasp. This hand position is the best way to not lose your pick in the context of strumming and picking.

Try strumming the strings of the guitar. Do not worry about placing your left hand for now. The part of your forearm that connects to the elbow should be used to stabilize the guitar against your body.

Right Hand Picking Posture

When you strum is important to remember to keep your forearm relaxed. The only pressure being applied during the strum should come from your fingers holding the pick in place. Imagine you are opening a door knob. Feel the way the arm stays stable from the elbow to the shoulder? This is the same mechanic you should apply to your strumming. DO NOT STRUM WITH THE ELBOW! The strumming needs to take place by turning the arm below the elbow.

Practice strumming in a downward direction followed by an upward direction. Try not to twist the angle of the pick too much as it should be hitting the strings directly on the flattest surface of the point of your pick. Attempt to only glide the tip of the pick across the top of the strings. If you dig in too deep, you will create greater resistance to your strum and a very jagged result sonically.

Pick Placement on the Strings

Practice strumming until you attain evenness in sound between the down strum and the up strum.

Left Hand Position

The left hand is known as the fretting hand. It is here that pitches are produced. We refer to the fingers as follows:

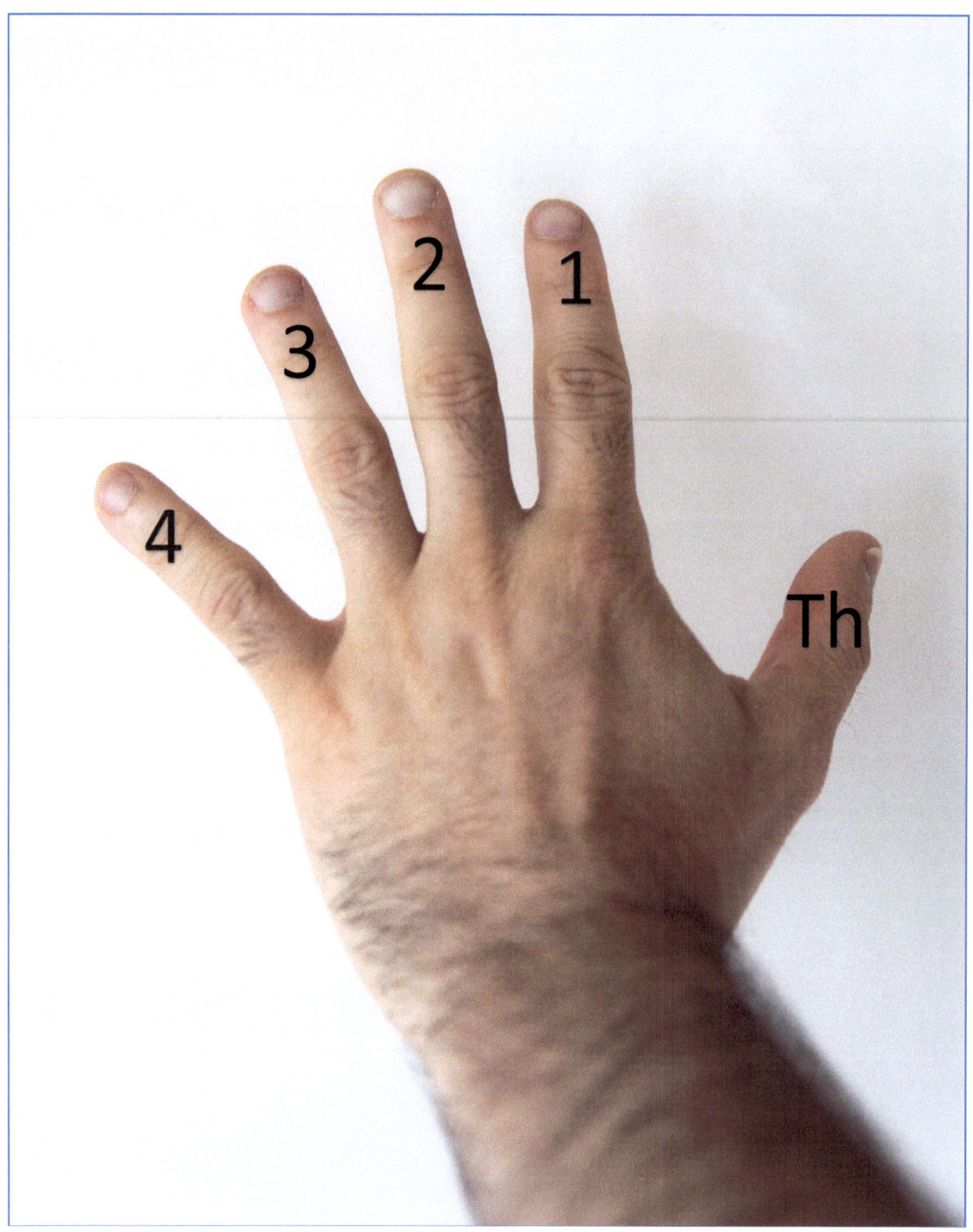

Image: Left hand with numbers (not actually tattooed on my hand!)

Left Hand Fingers:
1-*index*
2-*middle*
3-*ring*
4-*pinky*
Th-*thumb: very rarely used*

The fingers are numbered starting from the index finger. The thumb can be used to fret notes, in rare occasions. These occasions will not be covered in this book.

Left Hand thumb placement is one of the most crucial aspects (and most commonly mistaken in beginners) of guitar playing. The thumb is where all the counter balancing of pressure should come from when pressing down strings. To understand how the thumb should function try grabbing onto a desk or music stand. Pay close attention to how the thumb aligns with the rest of the fingers in this grip. Typically, the thumb ends up between the index and middle (first and second) fingers behind the object being grabbed. This is exactly how you should place your hand when it comes to playing single notes and chords on the guitar (although certain chords may require a slight altering to this position). Try this grip on your guitar now.

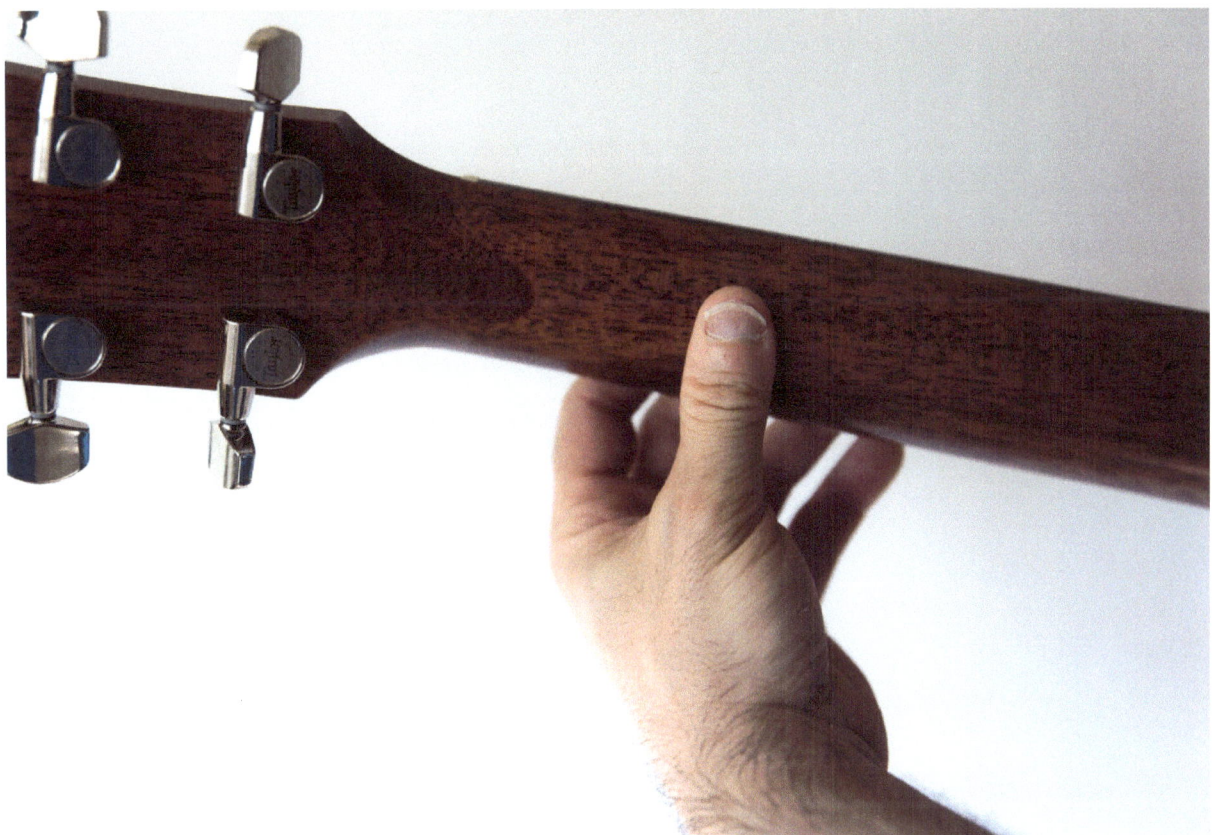

Correct thumb position

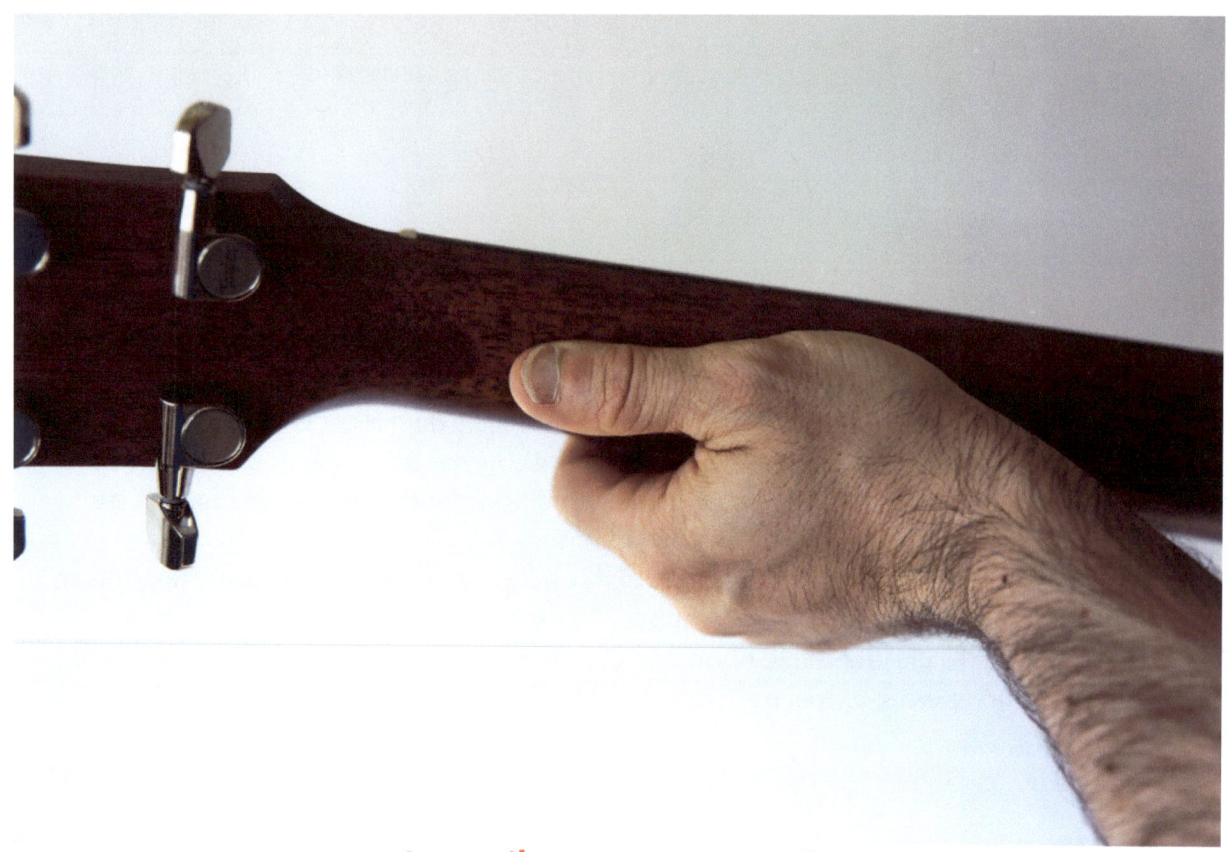

Incorrect! NO NO NO NO NO 🙅

Now let us try to fret a single note. Take your first finger and place it on the first fret of the first string. Keeping the thumb in its proper position, press down on the string using only your fingertip. In order for a pitch to be produced, the string must touch against the fret board. <u>Place the finger as close to the fret as possible, without being on top of the fret.</u> You should not see any of the fret wood between your finger and the fret. Conversely if you place your finger directly on top of the fret, you will hear a lot of buzz in your notes. If the string sounds dead, it most likely means you are not pressing down hard enough.

Correct placement of an F on the 1st string

WRONG!!!

When you start to learn chords, there may be some chords that render it physically impossible to have all of the fingers directly up to the edges of the frets, but you should always strive to place the fingers as high on the frets as possible even in these situations. You will attain a stronger and more accurate approach to guitar this way.

Fret Hand Exercise:

1) On the 1st string try to fret the first fret with the first finger. Pick downward on this single string.
2) Leaving the first finger in place, place the second finger on the second fret of the 1st string. Pick upward striking ONLY the 1st string.
3) Leaving both fingers in place, add the third finger to the third fret of the 1st string. Use a downstroke.
4) Place the fourth finger on the fourth fret of the 1st string, leaving all others in place. Make sure all fingers are up to the edges of the frets. Pick with and upstroke.
5) Repeat this across all of the other strings on the guitar.

Do this exercise as a daily warm up each time you start to practice.

Tuning

The guitar should be tuned every time you play. Different factors can affect the tuning of the guitar. Strings are made of metal and heat causes metal to expand. When the strings expand the pitch becomes lower. Over time wood body and neck of the guitar moves due to oxidation and other factors. This causes slight changes in the neck and can affect the guitar's intonation. Guitars subject to drastic temperature changes can be affected as well, for example, being outside with a guitar on a hot day and then bringing it inside a cool air-conditioned building. Finally, there is constant tension on the tuning pegs coming from the strings pulling on them all day. All tuning pegs eventually give in to the tension a bit over time (less expensive guitars tend to not stay in tune as well) and pitch can sink subtly.

But do not worry! Tuning the guitar is easy.

Electronic Tuners:

Electronic tuners are available as free downloads on your phone or device. There also may be some more advanced/accurate paid apps available. These apps function as a microphone and hear the pitch of your instrument and give you a readout of where your pitch stands in relation to standard A440 tuning. Clip-on tuners are very affordable and clip on to the headstock of your guitar tuning by sensing vibrations. Tuners also come as plug-in devices (stand-alone or foot pedals). These tend to be the most accurate and easy to use as you plug in a ¼ inch cable and the tuner senses the signal as the method of tuning.

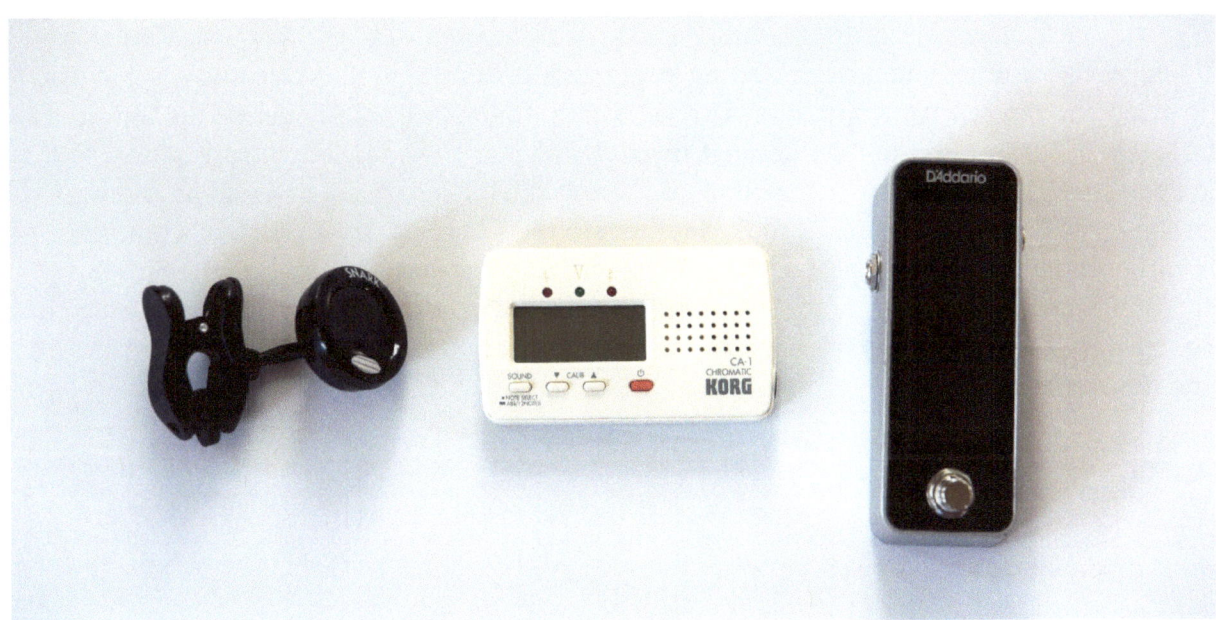

Left to Right: Clip-on, Stand-Alone, and Pedal Tuner

When tuning the guitar to an electronic tuner, the tuner will show you a digital meter and a pitch name. <u>Always make sure you are tuning the correct string to the correct pitch.</u> Remember:

E(6)-A(5)-D(4)-G(3)-B(2)-E(1)

When your pitch is in tune the meter will be straight up the center of the graph. Normally lights will come on to indicate that the string is tuned to pitch. Some tuners are chromatic (able to tune to any pitch) and some are just for guitar (will only find the pitches guitar strings should be tuned to). If your tuner is chromatic be careful you are not tuned to a pitch a half step below or above the note you want- for example: trying to tune an A and the tuner is reading A flat or G sharp.

If you find yourself twisting the tuning pegs and not hearing or seeing any difference in pitch, double check that you are adjusting the peg that corresponds to the string you are tuning. This is a common mistake that could lead to you overtightening and breaking a string.

Tuning by Ear:

Tuning by Ear assumes you have one string (preferable the low E) in tune already. You can use the piano or a reference pitch to tune the low E string. Then place your finger on the fifth fret of the low E (6th) string. Play that string, let it ring out, and play the open 5th string right next to it. An open string means you are not touching the string at all. These pitches should be identical. If not tune the 5th string until it does sound identical to the 6th string at the fifth fret. Continue this process on the next string set and the string set after. The one exception to the fifth fret placement is between the 3rd and 2nd strings. When you reach the 3rd string place your finger on the fourth fret to compare to the open 2nd string. Move back to the fifth fret of the 2nd string to tune the 1st string.

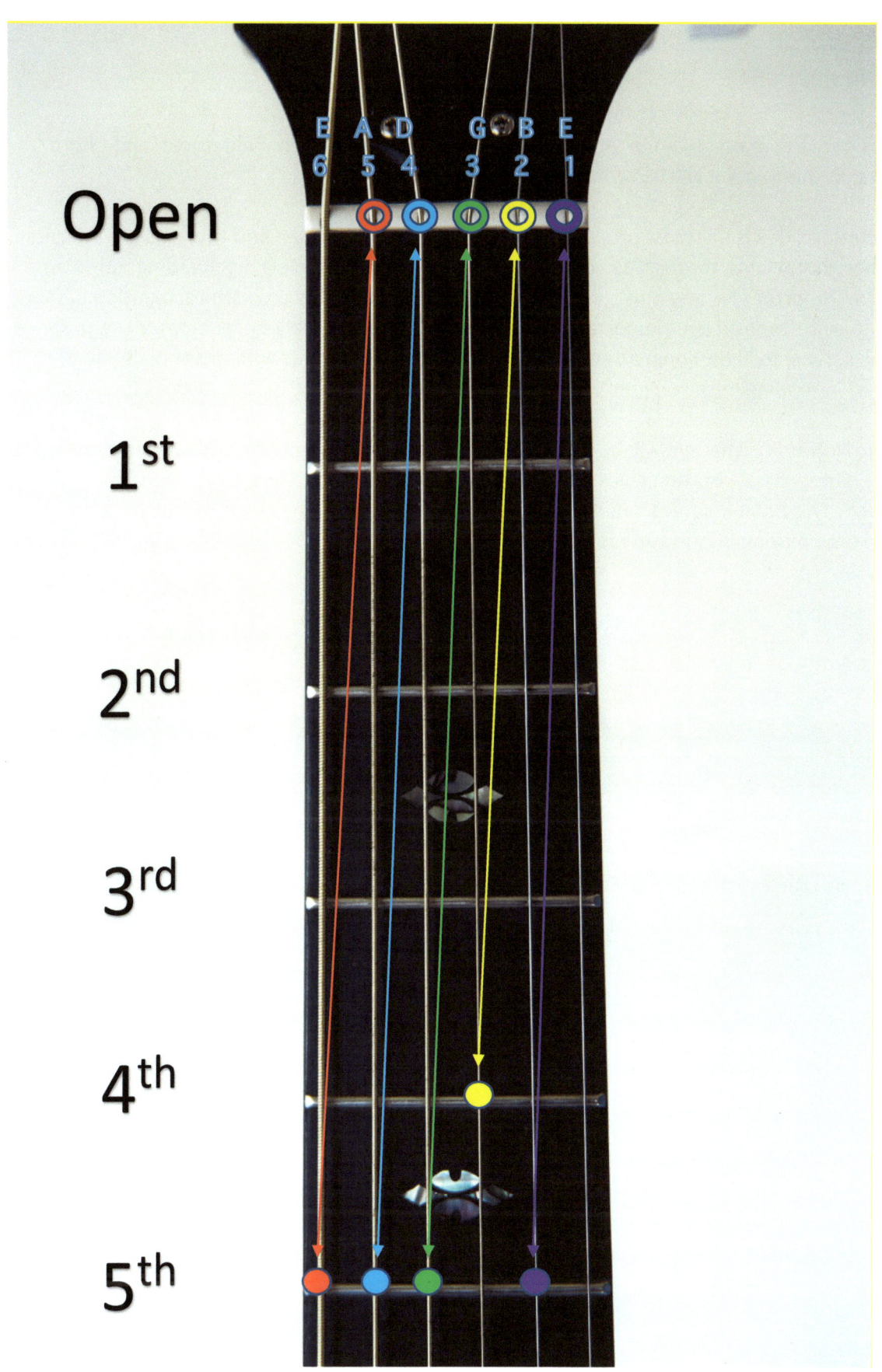

Guitar Nomenclature

There are three common ways of writing guitar music: Staff Notation, Tablatures, and Chord Diagrams. In this text we will use combinations of all three.

Staff Notation: This is the most proper form of writing music. Pitches and rhythms are indicated on five horizontal lines, through use of positioning, note heads, and stems. Reading music on the staff is important for any musicians, *however*, we will not focus on pitch recognition in this text. That is not to say it isn't important, but because it is not entirely necessary for the purpose this book serves; to allow songwriters to use the guitar as an accompaniment tool. If you are interested in reading music on guitar there are numerous other accessible sources to do so.

Rhythmic Notation: What we will be using as far as staff notation goes is slash and rhythmic notation. This type of notation gives you chord names and they rhythms that should be performed. This book assumes you have some knowledge of reading rhythms but will also provide some picking information for those that do not.

Rhythmic Notation looks like this:

Rhythmic Notation with chord symbols looks like this:

Tablature

Tablature or TABs is a simplified way to read guitar music. TAB staffs are made up of six horizontal lines. Each line is representative of one of the guitars strings with the low E (sixth string) being the bottom line and the high E (first string) being the top line.

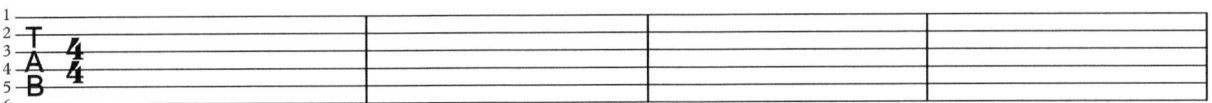

Numbers with rhythms will be written on the staff. The numbers indicate which fret of the given string will be played. The stems of the notes dictate which rhythms should be played. If the numbers are stacked, a chord is to be played. If the numbers are separate, they will sound one after the next. You may also see chord symbols above the TAB.

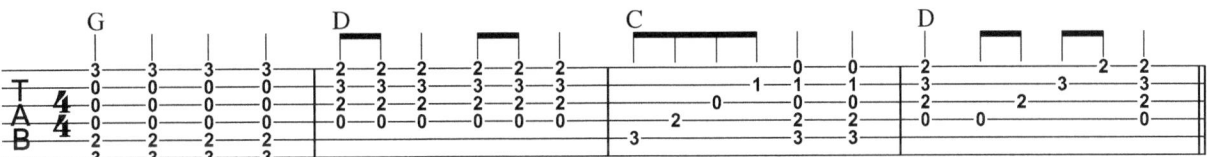

If no number is written on a string than the string should not sound.

The Pros and Cons of Each Notation Type

Staff Notation

Pros: By far the most comprehensive in terms of instructing the performer exactly what is to be played. Note names are shown by staff position. Easy to recognize combined notes and rhythms. Fingerings can be included with each pitch.

Cons: Time consuming to learn.

Rhythmic Notation

Pros: Provides the minimum information to perform a selection, making for the easiest way to begin.

Cons: Assumes you know which chord shapes to play. Not able to show specific parts such as arpeggiation or single note phrases.

Tablature

Pros: Able to demonstrate exact parts. Easy to learn.

Cons: Will not tell you what note names are. Not transferrable to non-fretted instruments. Will often not show you what fingers to use.

Chord Diagrams

Chord diagrams are the quickest and easiest way to learn the fingerings for new guitar chords. Chord diagrams represent a view of your guitar neck as if you were looking at the guitar facing right back at you.

Similar to our tuning diagram, the vertical lines represent the strings from left to right:

6-5-4-3-2-1

The thick horizontal line represents the nut and the subsequent horizontal lines represent each fret 1-5. If a number appears to the left side of a chord diagram, shift to the indicated fret and align the spacing from there. For example, if a 5 appears to the left of the diagram the first line after the nut would represent the 5th fret, the next line the 6th fret, then the 7th and so on.

Dots on the diagram will indicate which strings and frets the fingers are to be placed on. The numbers inside the dots represent which left hand fingers to use. 'O' above any string indicates the string should be open (untouched). An 'X' above any string suggests the string should not be sounded at all in the chord.

It is time to learn our first chord. Here is a diagram for an E minor (Em) open chord.

Em:

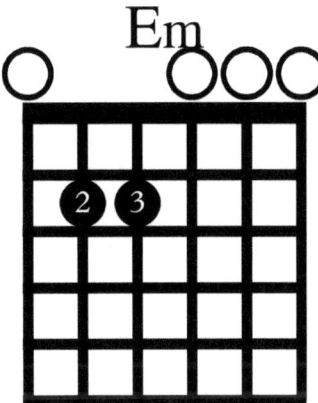

1. Place the second finger on the second fret of the 5th string
2. Place the third finger behind it on the second fret of the 4th string
3. Pluck each string from the 6th to the 1st, one at a time to make sure all pitches sound

Troubleshooting chord issues:

If any notes are not ringing clearly try to identify what the problem is.
-Are you pressing down on the strings hard enough?
-Is your finger pressing down right on top of the fret rather than directly behind it?
-Is the fleshy part of one of your fingers slightly touching an adjacent string?

In the initial stages of learning chords it is very important to play each individual string to check if all of the notes are sounding clearly. It is easy to miss a dead note if you strum through an entire chord. Always check! Eventually your fingers will retain muscle memory and always go to the exact spots they have been trained to find. Make sure to train them to find the correct spots or you will have to go back and re-learn chords.

<u>Remember the difference between a full sounding chord and a chord with dead notes are very subtle. Even a fraction of a fingering position adjustment can make a big difference in sound quality.</u>

How to practice new chords:

After placing fingers and spot checking each note, take your fingers away from the neck while leaving the thumb in place. Completely straighten your fingers and reform the chord shape. The goal is to have your fingers find the shape simultaneously, moving in conjunction and not one at a time. If each finger has to find its position separately from the others, it will take that much longer to perform chord switches. Make your fingers move as a team by practicing the mechanics at a snail's 🐌 pace. Force them to move the way you want and in time they will respond quicker.

Let's learn our second chord.

Am:

1. Place the second finger on the second fret of the 4th string
2. Place the third finger behind it on the second fret of the 3rd string
3. Place the first finger on the first fret of the 2nd string
4. Pluck each string from the 5th to the 1st, one at a time to make sure all pitches sound
5. Remember to avoid the 6th string in this chord

Chord switching:

Practice both the Em and the Am individually first using the method provided above. Now practice going in between the two chord shapes. Shift back and forth making sure to pick each string individually to check note clarity. Focus on proper finger placement and moving your fingers as a group rather than individually as you bounce between the chords.

Once you are comfortable moving between the chords try this exercise:

Strum all chords four times in a downward direction.

Focus on not slowing down your tempo to switch to the next chord.

Repeat over and over until consistent.

The symbols at the beginning and end of this example are called **repeat signs**. *At this stage of your practicing it is important to repeat things as much as you can before you have to throw up 🤮. This type of repetition is key to being able to "program" your hands to what you need them to do on the guitar.*

When you feel comfortable, try switching the chords twice as fast:

C:

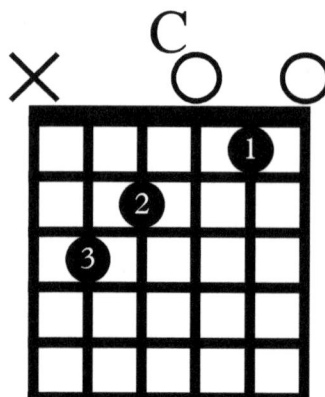

1. Place the third finger on the third fret of the 5th string
2. Place the second finger behind it on the second fret of the 4th string
3. Place the first finger on the first fret of the 2nd string
4. Pluck each string from the 5th to the 1st, one at a time to make sure all pitches sound
5. Remember to avoid the 6th string in this chord

Or:

1. Play an Am
2. Remove the third finger from the second fret of the 3rd string while keeping other fingers pressed down
3. Place the third finger on the third fret of the 5th string
4. Remember to avoid the 6th string in this chord

It is important to notice that the C shape shares two of the same fingers with the Am shape. By minimizing the fingers that need to be switched, chord switching can be much smoother.

Troubleshooting the C chord:

-Is your third finger arched so as to avoid contact with the 4th string?
-Is your first finger on an "island" so as not to make contact with the 3rd or 1st strings?
-Are you using proper thumb placement on the back of the neck to allow the fingers to arch properly?

Try these exercises moving only the third finger. Repeat over and over.

1.3 C   Am   C   Am

Remember to strum downward without breaking pace when you switch chords.

1.4 Am C Am C Am C Am C

G:

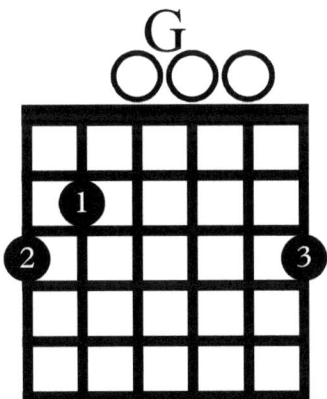

1. Place the second finger on the third fret of the 6th string
2. Place the first finger behind it on the second fret of the 5th string
3. Place the third finger on the third fret of the 1st string
4. Pluck each string from the 6th to the 1st, one at a time to make sure all pitches sound

Troubleshooting the G chord:

-Is your second finger arched so as to avoid contact with the 5th string?
-Is your first finger arched so as not to make contact with the 4th string?
-Are you using proper thumb placement on the back of the neck to allow the fingers to arch properly?

The G to C switch is an extremely common occurrence in pop music. Spend time perfecting this switch. Then try these progressions:

D:

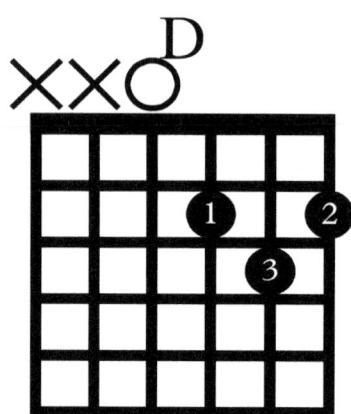

1. Place the first finger on the second fret of the 3rd string
2. Place the third finger behind it on the third fret of the 2nd string
3. Place the second finger behind it on the second fret of the 1st string
4. Pluck each string from the 4th to the 1st, one at a time to make sure all pitches sound
5. Remember to avoid the both the 5th and 6th strings in this chord

-Is your third finger on an "island" so as not to make contact with the 3rd or 1st strings?
-Are you using proper thumb placement on the back of the neck to allow the fingers to arch properly?
-Are you strumming the correct amount of strings (4 only)?

Try these exercises:

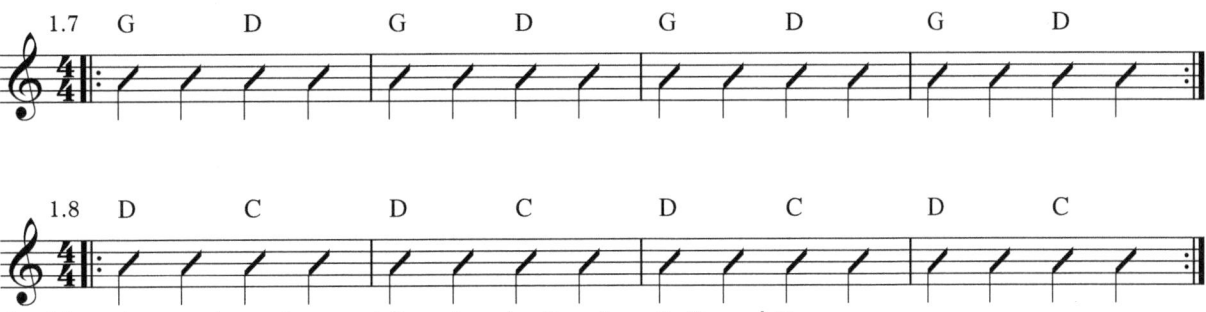

At this point you have learned five chords: Em, Am, C, G, and D.

Review:

Try taking any combination of two chords and switching in between. Again, check your individual strings. Try to memorize the shapes and move your fingers are a group rather than individually. The more time you spend doing these types of exercises, the quicker your development will be.

Chapter 1 Practice Progressions:

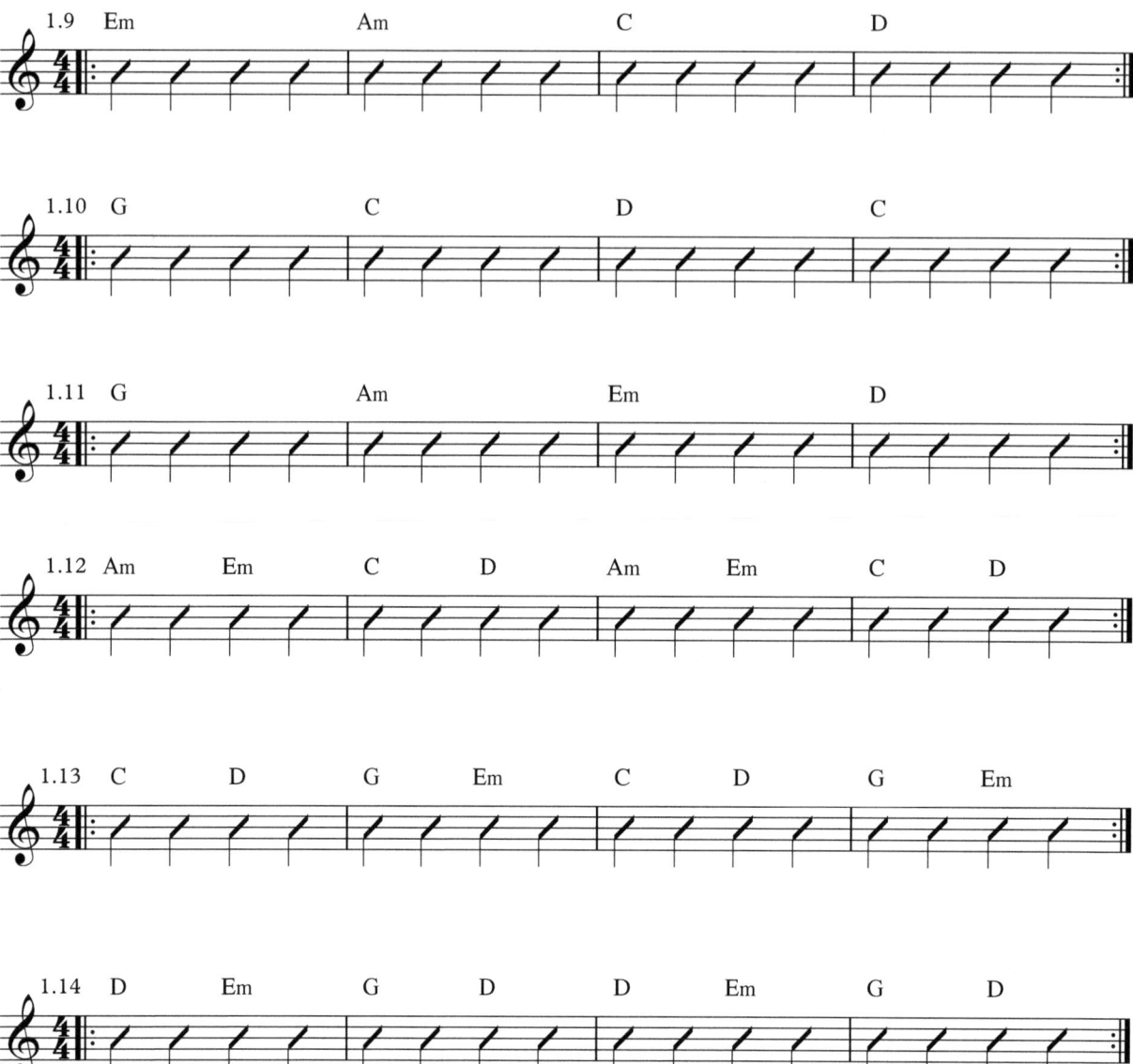

56

Chapter 2: Open Chords and Strum Patterns

Up to this point we have only focused on quarter note rhythms, strummed with downstrokes. In this chapter we will now include off beat rhythms played with an upstrokes.

We know that quarter notes get one beat. And in a bar of 4/4 we will play any count of "1", "2", "3" or "4" with a downstoke.

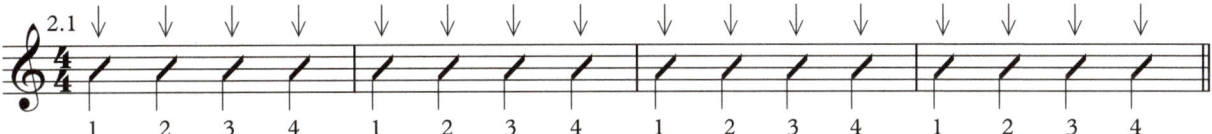

Even if quarter note rests (beats of silence) were included, the picking direction would not change.

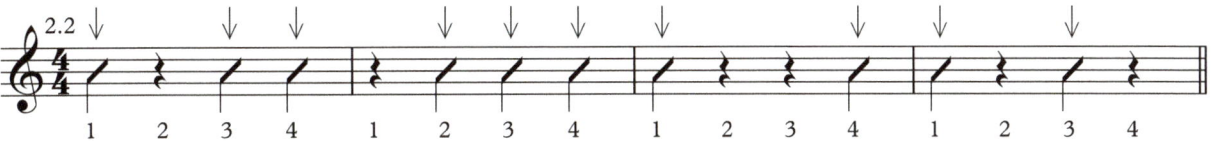

Try strumming this pattern on an open G chord. Make sure to silence 🤫 the strings during the rest by lightly touching against them with the palm of your right hand after the strum. The counts are now removed.

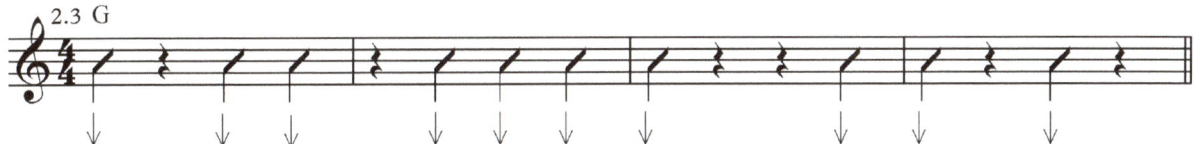

Now let us add the notes in between the beats. A series of 8th notes will require alternate (down-up-down-up) picking.

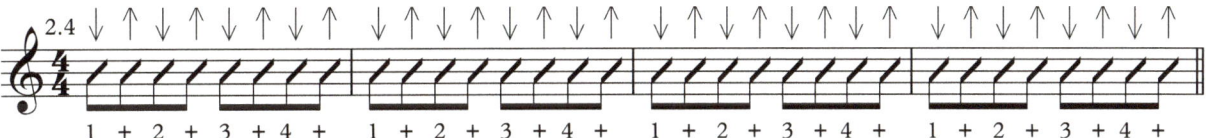

Practice alternate strumming on a G chord. Try to maintain and even attack on the upwards motion. Try to glide the tip of the pick along the tops of the strings. If you dig too far into the strings you will meet resistance from the string causing a less smooth sound. Keep the wrist loose!

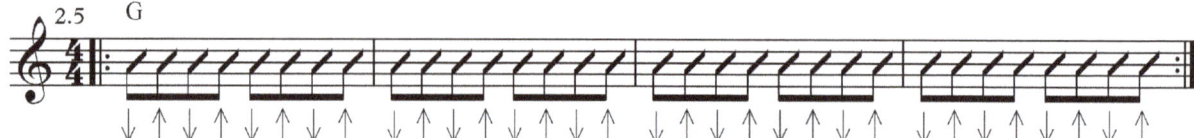

The concept of this picking exercise is one of the most vital things you can practice. Keep the down and upstrokes even and get a feel for the steadiness of moving the right hand in this rhythm. This motion will be present even when you are not playing each 8th note. Try performing this rhythm with a C chord.

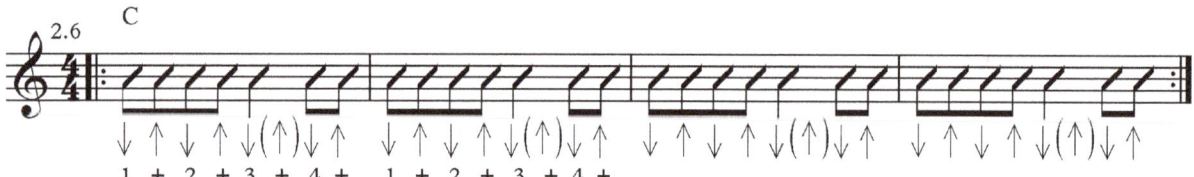

The notes in parenthesis should still be strummed, but in the air <u>without</u> making contact with the strings. This will allow for you to maintain a solid groove as you **subdivide** each 8th note in the measure evenly. The concept of subdivision refers to the process of counting the smallest rhythmic value in each measure, even when those smaller rhythms are not being used. In these examples, count out all 8th notes in the measure even when a quarter note rhythm is being performed. This may take some getting used to, but worth starting on right away.

<u>Helpful hint: You should always pick in a downwards direction on rhythms placed on the down-beats (1 2 3 4) and an upwards direction on notes placed in between the beats (+).</u>

Some chords require strumming fewer than the full six strings of the guitar. Make sure you do not strum any open strings that should not be in the chord! I would advise on your upstroke to aim for one less string than required as your momentum is likely to carry you into the next string. On the C chord for example, aim to stop at the 4th string. Your momentum will want to propel into the 5th string which is still used in the chord. If you don't follow this strategy you will probably play the 6th string in your strum, a note that should be avoided in this particular chord.

Learn to equivalate rhythm groups with pick directions:

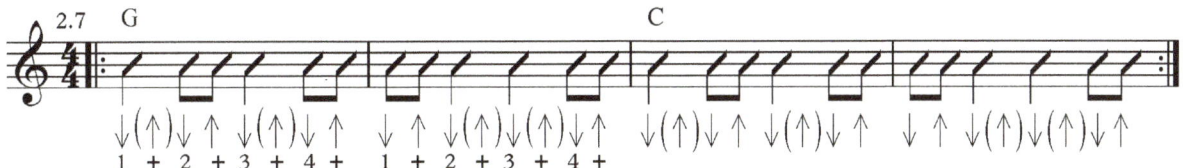

Take care to only hit five strings in the C chord while hitting all six in the G chord.

This next exercise will demonstrate off beat emphasis:

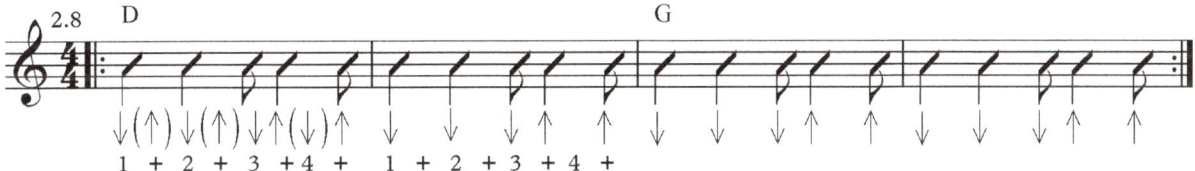

Every rhythm in this example should be played identically. Even though the parenthesis strum directions disappear in the second measure, they should still be played in the air.

Try to figure out the pick directions in the following example:

Rests

Just as it is notated when to play, it is also notated when to silence your strings. These notation are called **rests** 😴. Figuring out how long a rest lasts is pretty simple. Rests occur for the same length as their counterparts. The example below contains **quarter note rests**, a squiggly line that tells you to not make any noise for one beat.

Remember your hand must continue its down-up-down-up momentum even during rests:

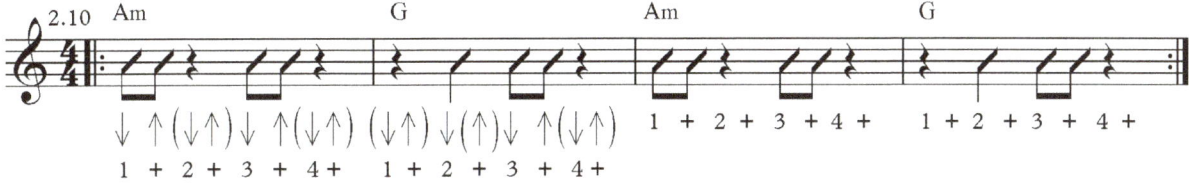

Keep in mind you need to stop the sound of the chords during rests by silencing the strings with the palm of your right hand. It's important to continue alternating your right hand up and down while you do so. This may be difficult at first. Remember that you barely need to touch the strings to get the sound to stop. Do not exaggerate the motion as it will take you out of the flow of your right hand's trajectory.

E:

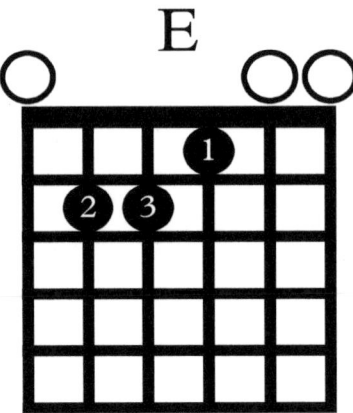

1. Place the second finger on the second fret of the 5th string
2. Place the third finger behind it on the second fret of the 4th string
3. Place the first finger on the first fret of the 3rd string
4. Pluck each string from the 6th to the 1st, one at a time to make sure all pitches sound

Or:

1. Play an Em
2. Add the first finger to the first fret of the 3rd string

Try these exercises using the new E chord shape:

Don't forget to use the proper picking directions!

When moving from the E back to the Am chord, notice how the fingering is identical. Try to keep your hand shape maintained and just slide everything over to the next set of strings (avoiding the 6th string on the Am strum of course). The less you move your hand, the quicker the changes will be.

E7:

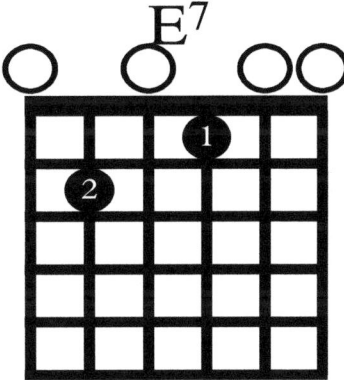

1. Place the second finger on the second fret of the 5th string
2. Place the first finger on the first fret of the 3rd string
3. Pluck each string from the 6th to the 1st one at a time to make sure all pitches sound

Or:

1. Play an E
2. Remove the third finger from the 4th string

Troubleshooting the E7 chord:

-Is your second finger arched so as to avoid contact with the 4th string?

Another reminded to only strum the number of strings required for each chord.

A:

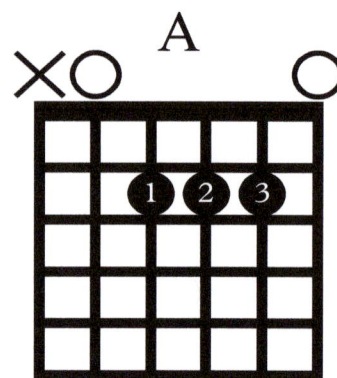

1. Place the third finger on the second fret of the 2nd string
2. Place the second finger in front of it on the second fret of the 3rd string
3. Place the first finger in front of it on the second fret of the 5th string
4. Pluck each string from the 5th to the 1st, one at a time to make sure all pitches sound
5. Remember to avoid the 6th string in this chord

Notice how this chord was built backwards from chords we learned previously 🤔? This is to help squeeze the fingers closer to the edges of each fret.

Troubleshooting the A chord:

-Are all of your fingers up as close as they can be to the edges of the frets?

Think "down-up-up-down-down" as you play:

Don't forget to silence your strings while maintaining your momentum during rests.

A7:

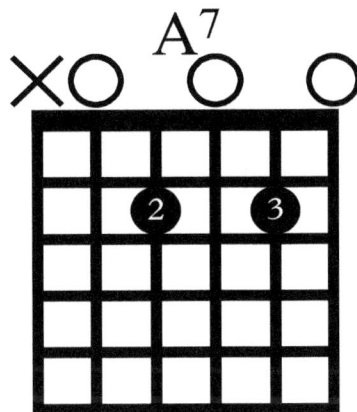

1. Place the second finger on the second fret of the 4th string
2. Place the third finger on the second fret of the 2nd string
3. Pluck each string from the 5th to the 1st, one at a time to make sure all pitches sound clearly
4. Remember to avoid the 6th string in this chord

Troubleshooting the A7 chord:

-Is your second finger muting the open 3rd string?

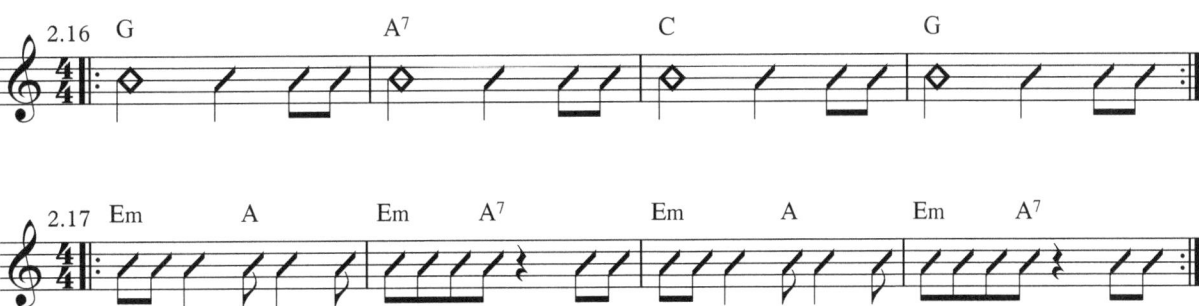

In exercise 2.17, notice that the chord changes to the A7 on the "+" of two in both the second and fourth measures. The A7 should be played with the upstroke of your pick and then silenced shortly after for the rest on beat 3. You might also consider forming the Em chord in bar 1 with the first and second fingers to allow for an easier shift to the A7 that follows.

63

Dm:

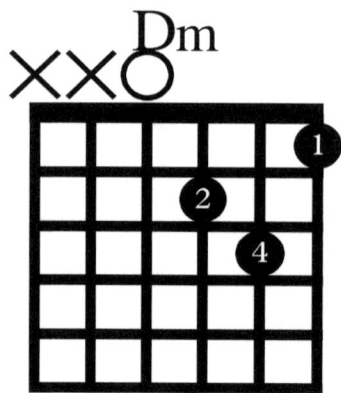

1. Place the second finger on the second fret of the 3rd string
2. Place the fourth finger behind it on the third fret of the 2nd string
3. Place the first finger behind it on the first fret of the 1st string
4. Pluck each string from the 4th to the 1st, one at a time to make sure all pitches sound clearly
5. Remember to avoid the 6th and 5th strings in this chord

Troubleshooting the Dm chord:

-Is your fourth finger muting the 1st string?
-Is your fourth finger properly arched and applying enough pressure?

When the chord switches from E to E7 simply lift off your third finger while leaving the other two fingers in place.

Make sure the chord sounds on the "+" of 4 before switching to the chord in the next measure.

G7:

1. Place the third finger on the third fret of the 6th string
2. Place the second finger behind it on the second fret of the 5th string
3. Place the first finger on the first fret of the 1st string
4. Pluck each string from the 6th to the 1st, one at a time to make sure all pitches sound clearly

Troubleshooting the G7 chord:

-Is your third finger muting the 5th string?
-Is your second finger muting the 4th string?
-Is your first finger properly placed and applying enough pressure?

Don't fall into the rhythm trap in bar 4 🙀!

D7:

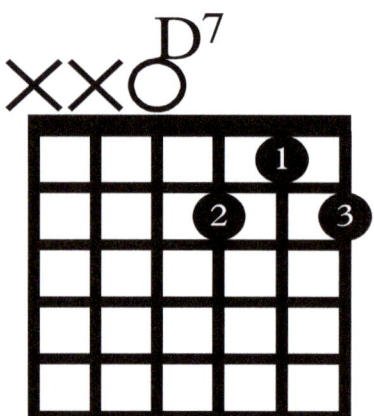

1. Place the second finger on the second fret of the 3rd string
2. Place the first finger behind it on the first fret of the 2nd string
3. Place the third finger behind it on the second fret of the 1st string
4. Pluck each string from the 4th to the 1st, one at a time to make sure all pitches sound clearly
5. Remember to avoid the 6th and 5th strings in this chord

Troubleshooting the D7 chord:

-Is your second finger muting the 2nd string?
-Are you playing the D chord by mistake? The D7 looks like an upside-down D 🙃.

*This example contains two **8th note rests**. They occur on the first beat of measures 1 and 3. They looks like fancy 🖌 7's and would require you to not play for half of a beat. Come in on the + of beat 1 with an upstroke.

Chapter 2 Practice Progressions:

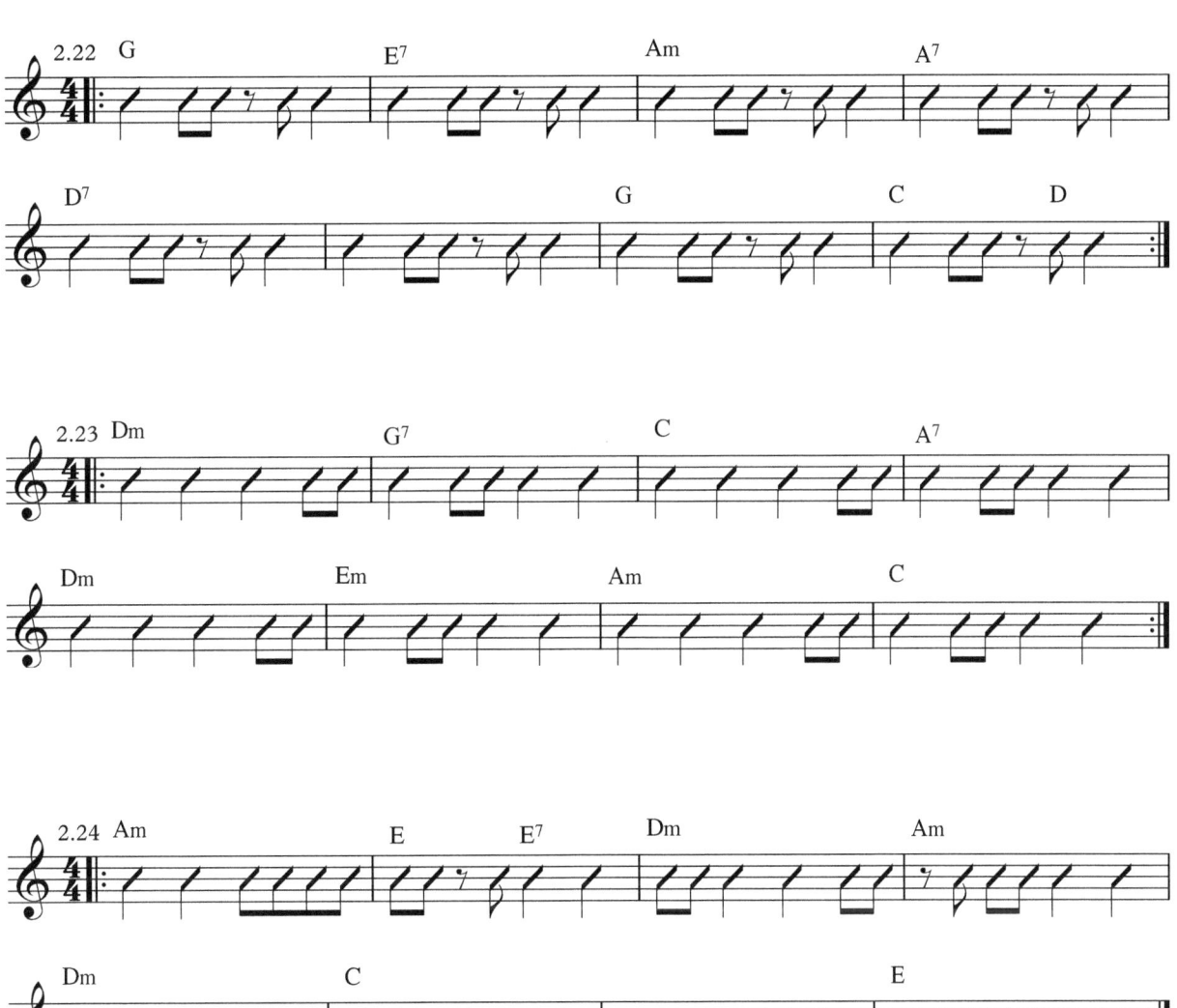

Chapter 3: More Open Chords and Syncopated Strum Patterns

In this chapter we will examine **syncopation** which describes rhythmic groupings that stress "weak" beats. The stresses in eighth note syncopation tend to be on the "+". **Ties** are used to hold note values over barlines and other areas when a strong downbeat would feel natural to emphasize. Think of ties as you would a plus (+) sign in mathematics. The tie symbols adds the lengths of the two indicated note values together.

For example: A quarter note tied to an 8th note holds for one and a half beats. A dotted quarter tied to an 8th note holds for two beats total.

In this example of syncopated rhythm, you would only attack the strings on the slash before the tie. The sound carries through the length of the tie and you would not play again until the next non-tied note. As with the strum patterns found in the last chapter, you will always pick in a downwards direction on rhythms placed on the down-beats (1 2 3 4) and an upwards direction on notes placed in between the beats (+). Remember to keep your right hand moving in a perpetual down-up-down-up motion, removing the pick from the strings when attacks are not required. This will help you count the rhythms better as you coordinate the down and up of your foot with the down and up motion of your hand.

The picking for the previous example would look like this:

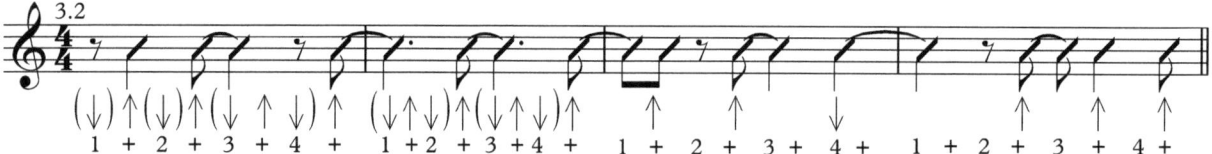

The arrows in parenthesis have been removed in the third and fourth measures but the right hand should continue its flow focusing on the number of attacks per measure. This example has only two or three attacks per bar. If you simplify accordingly, it makes a seemingly complicated rhythm easier to process. When counting the following examples, make a note of what pick directions will hit the strings before you begin playing.

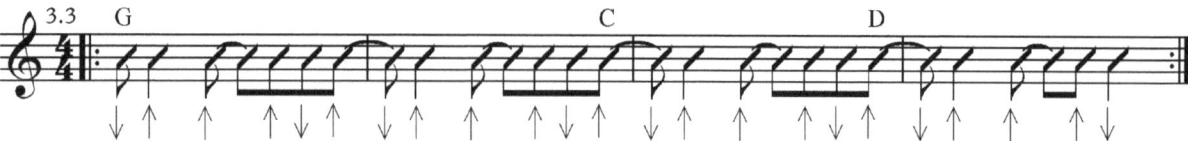

You will need to change to the C and D chords on the "+" of four. This early chord change is common in syncopated rhythms and is known as **anticipation**.

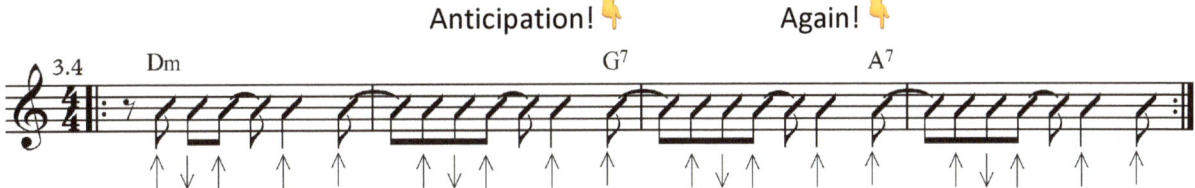

Pay close attention to when the chords change.

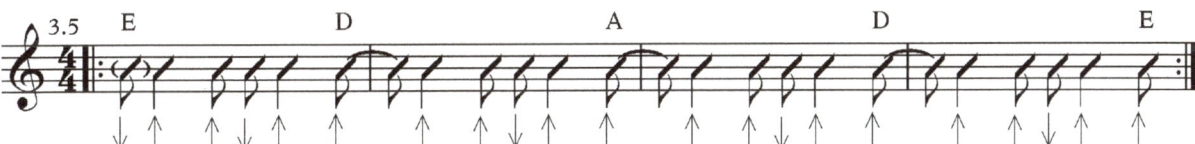

This example contains a different rhythm in the first and second bars which repeat in identical fashion in the third and fourth bars. The E chord at the end will tie into beat one on the repeat. You should NOT reattack the E on beat one of the repeat.

Counting 16th Note Rhythms

Within a quarter note there is space for two 8th notes.
Within two 8th notes there is space for four 16th notes.

A 16th note breaks down similar to an 8th note performed at twice the speed, as an 8th note breaks down as a quarter note performed at twice the speed.

16th notes are counted as "1 e + a, 2 e + a, 3 e + a, 4 e + a". The +'s will land in the same place in the measure as they would if you were counting 8th notes. The e's and a's will land evenly between the downbeat and the "+".

Picking Directions for 16th Note Rhythmic Groupings

As with 8th notes, 16th notes will be alternate picked:

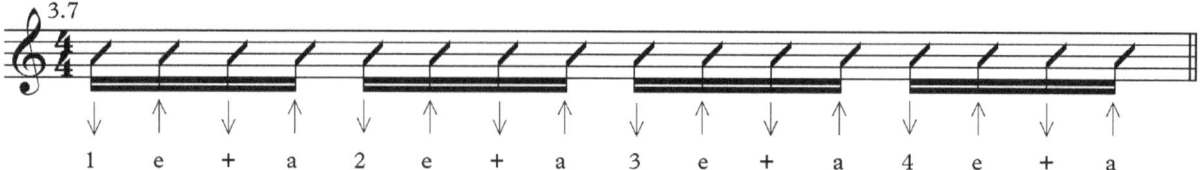

When 8th notes are combined with 16th notes, there are two options for picking:

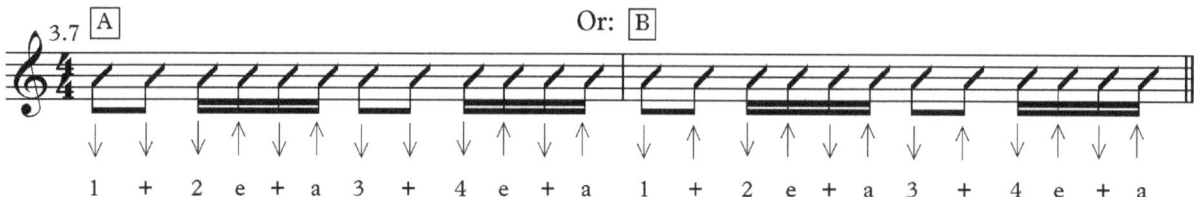

Option A:

The advantage of option A is the 8th notes are now all picked with down strokes consistently across the entire measure. I would recommend this approach in most situations.

Option B:

The advantage of option B is that the 8th notes are picked with the same directions that we used in examples containing only quarter and 8th notes. You would double your picking speed when you encountered 16th notes. I would suggest this approach on faster tempos.

Here are the recommended picking directions for various rhythmic groupings that combine 8th and 16th notes:

As with the 8th note concept, the right hand would continue its down-up-down-up momentum during held notes, moving the pick on and off the strings.

Try some practice progressions using the groupings we have examined so far:

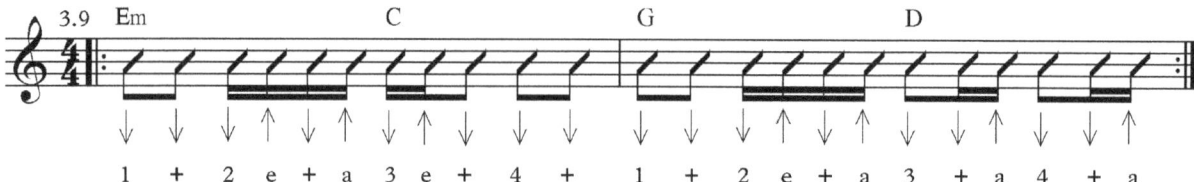

70

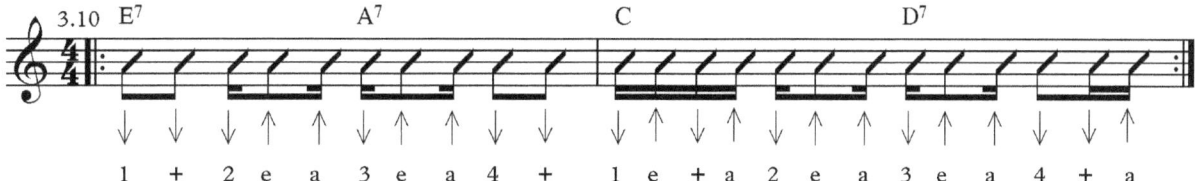

Try the same progression with ties:

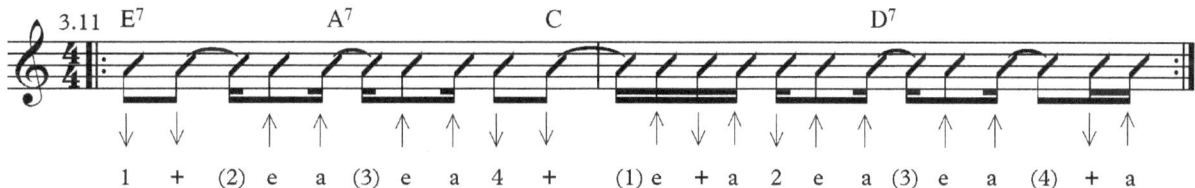

Make sure to anticipate the coming chords. Be sure to differentiate between the 8th and 16th note anticipations.

Try to figure out the counting yourself this time:

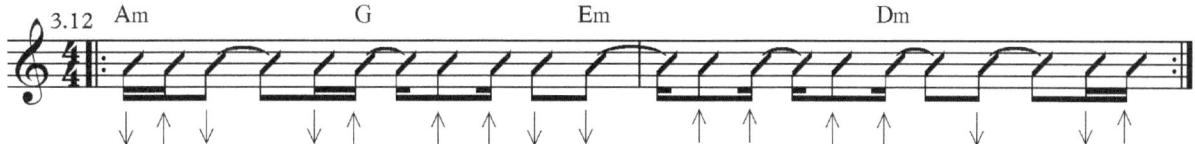

Remember that when rhythms become difficult, the best procedure is to slow down the tempo to the point you have time to process what needs to be played. Practicing too quickly will be frustrating and actually be more harmful than helpful. Rhythmic accuracy is important to develop from these initial stages.

B7:

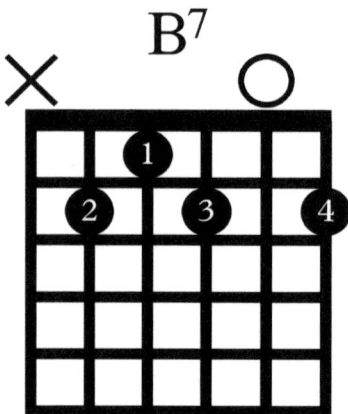

1. Place the second finger on the second fret of the 5th string
2. Place the first finger behind it on the first fret of the 4th string
3. Place the third finger behind it on the second fret of the 3rd string
4. Place the fourth finger on the second fret of the 1st string
5. Pluck each string from the 5th to the 1st, one at a time to make sure all pitches sound

Troubleshooting the B7 chord:

-Are all four fingers pressing down with enough strength?
-Is your third finger muting the 2nd string?
-Are you accidentally playing the open 6th string?

When changing from Em to B7, do not remove your second finger as it is in the same position for both chords.

When changing from B7 to Am, do not remove your third finger as it is in the same position for both chords (same goes for the return to the B7).

C7:

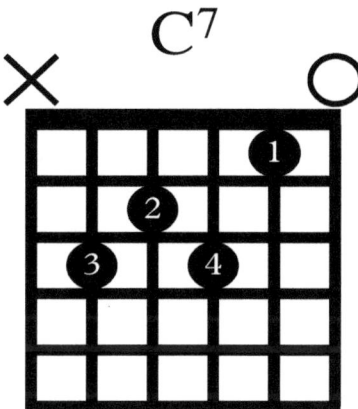

1. Place the third finger on the third fret of the 5th string
2. Place the second finger behind it on the second fret of the 4th string
3. Place the fourth finger behind it on the third fret of the 3rd string
4. Place the first finger on the first fret of the 2nd string
5. Pluck each string from the 5th to the 1st, one at a time to make sure all pitches sound
6. Remember to avoid the 6th string in this chord

Or:

1. Play a C
2. Place the fourth finger on the third fret of the 3rd string
3. Remember to avoid the 6th string in this chord

Troubleshooting the C7 chord:

-Is your third finger flattening to the point where it is muting the 4th string?
-Is your fourth finger pressed down hard enough?

Try working on the chord switches and picking pattern separately at first. With new chords and new rhythms it is more effective to separate the practice elements.

Asus2:

1. Place the second finger on the second fret of the 4th string
2. Place the third finger behind it on the second fret of the 3rd string
3. Pluck each string one at a time from the 5th to the 1st to make sure all the pitches sound
4. Remember to avoid the 6th string in this chord

Or:

1. Play an Amin
2. Remove the first finger
3. Pluck each string from the 5th to the 1st, one at a time to make sure all pitches sound

Dsus2:

1. Place the first finger on the second fret of the 3rd string
2. Place the third finger behind it on the third fret of the 2nd string
3. Pluck each string from the 4th to the 1st, one at a time to make sure all pitches sound
4. Remember to avoid the both the 5th and 6th strings in this chord

Or:

1. Play a D chord
2. Remove the second finger
3. Pluck each string from the 4th to the 1st, one at a time to make sure all pitches sound

Mark in the pick directions ∕ if the rhythm seems tricky.

Cadd9:

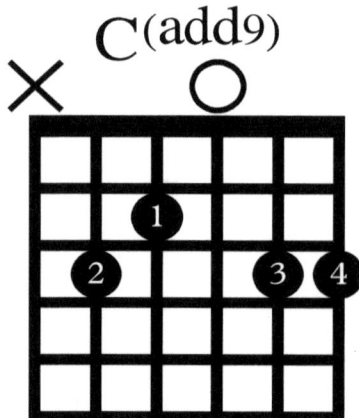

1. Place the second on the third fret of the 5th string
2. Place the first finger behind it on the second fret of the 4th string
3. Place the third finger on the third fret of the 2nd string
4. Place the fourth finger behind it on the third fret of the 1st string
5. Pluck each string from the 5th to the 1st, one at a time to make sure all pitches sound
6. Remember to avoid the 6th string in this chord

Troubleshooting the Cadd9 chord:

-Is your second finger arched enough to avoid contact with the 4th string?
-Is your first finger positioned so as to avoid contact with the open 3rd string?

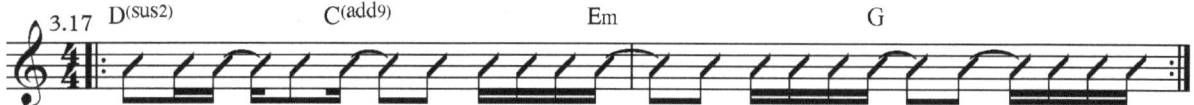

Chapter 3 Practice Progressions:

Drawing from all the chords you have learned so far, try coming up with interesting chord progressions to match the following rhythm patterns. Experiment with different orders, returning to chords previously used, and placing changes on anticipations.

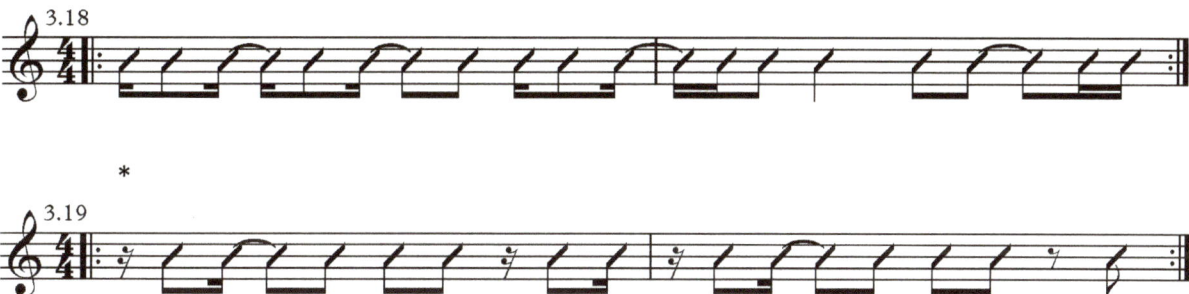

*The new symbol on beats 1 and four of this bar is the 16th note rest. Figure out how to count it by accounting for the remaining beats in the measure 🕵.

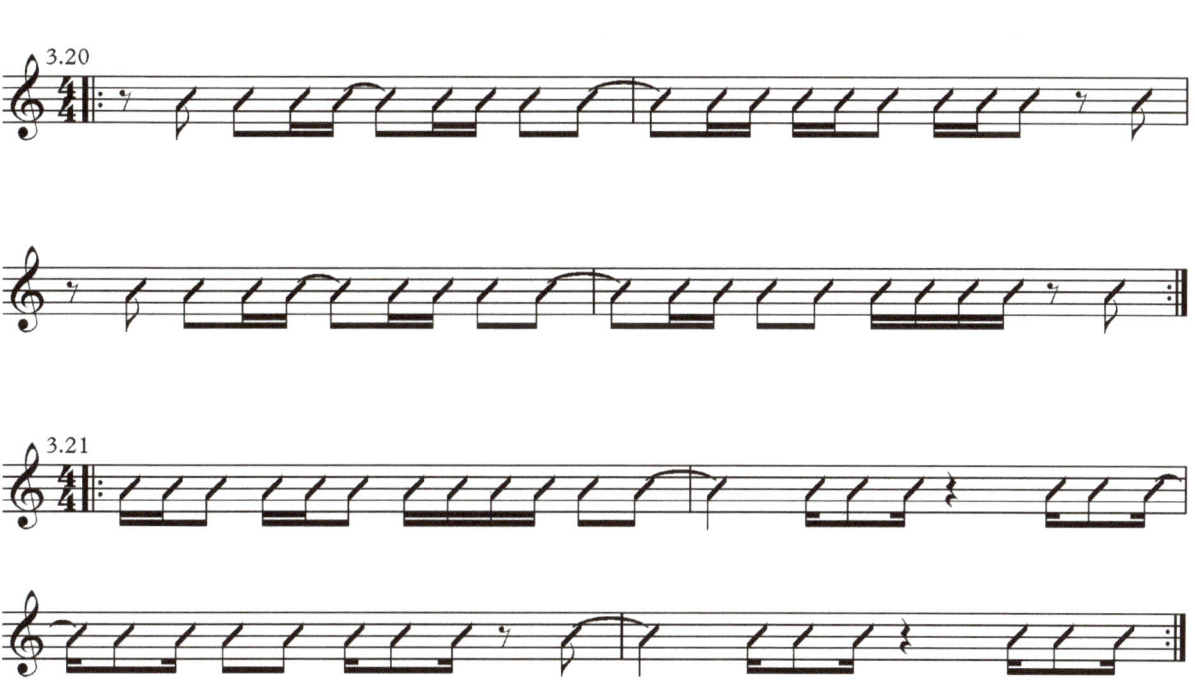

Chapter 4: Progression Creation, Transposition and Arpeggiation

It is now time to take the chords we have learned to this point and try to create our own progressions. It is quite helpful to understand basic diatonic harmony in order to know how to combine chords in a musical fashion. I want to stress that although theory is very helpful for creating progressions, it should not be your only method of writing. Make sure to experiment with the sounds of the chords first and foremost. You might come up with a fantastic sounding series of chords that most music theorists would frown upon 😵. Diatonic harmony is a great way to get started composing chord progressions but always look for a unique chord or switch to make your song stand out on its own merits.

Major Scale Diatonic Harmony

All analysis of diatonic harmony derives from a major scale. The major scale is constructed upon the following formula of half steps (1 fret on the guitar) and whole steps (2 frets on the guitar).

Whole-Whole-Half-Whole-Whole-Whole-Half

Or in terms of fret spacing:

2-2-1-2-2-2-1

If you start on any notes and consider that the tonic (beginning) of the scale and ascend the frets in that order you will be preforming a major scale.

Here is a major scale in the key of C:

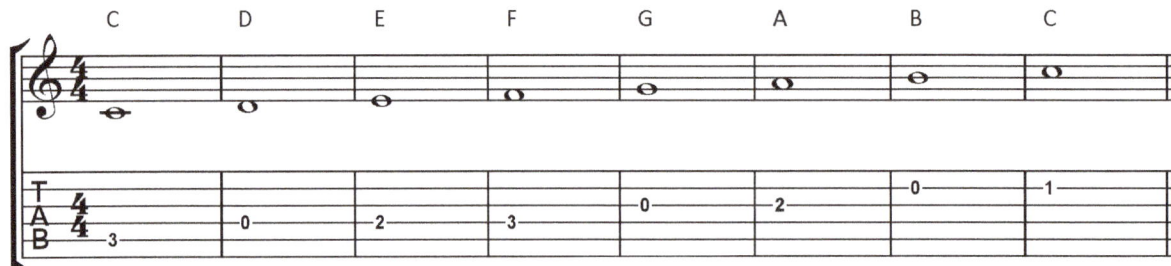

Consider each degree of the scale as a number; C=1, D=2, E=3, F=4, G=5, A=6, B=7

When we return to the C (or octave), the process starts again.

In order to harmonize the scale we will stack the notes in 3rds. Think of it as skipping over a scale degree and adding the next note, and repeating the process.

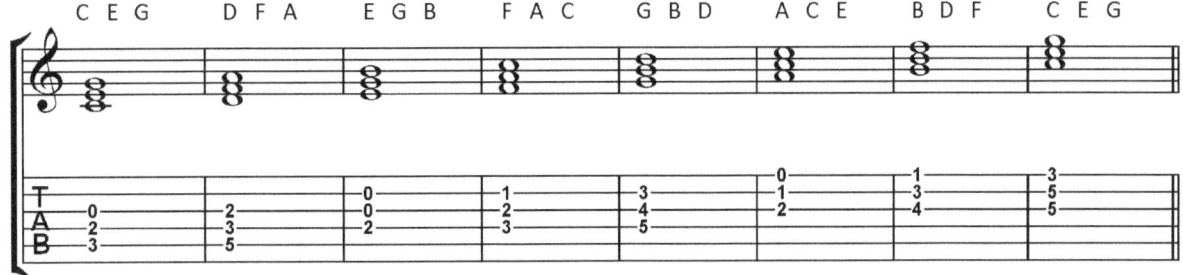

Now we will label each chord by its proper title:

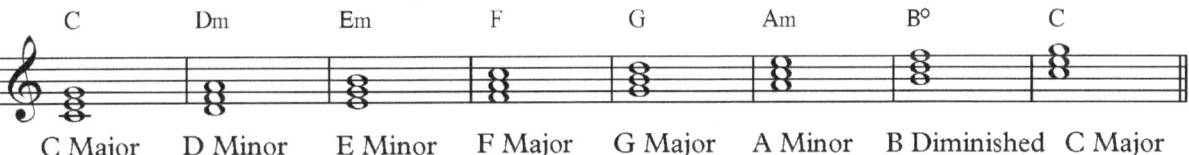

This harmonization of the major scale must then be applied to other keys as well. In order to organize it into a system that will translate to any key we assign Roman numerals to each chord. An uppercase Roman numeral indicates a major chord while a lowercase Roman numeral indicates a minor sound.

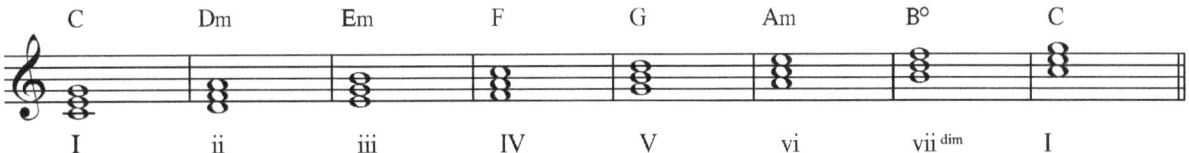

The vii[th] chord of the harmonization, the diminished triad, is seldom used in popular or rock music. The flat VII major is the most common substitute.

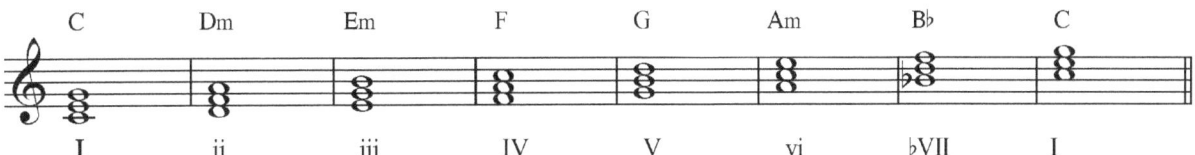

As a songwriter, it is helpful to know common substitutes for diatonic harmony. This will help make your progressions a little less predictable. Another interesting substitute found in Country music is to replace any of the minor chords in the progression (and the V major and flat VII major) with dominant 7 chords.

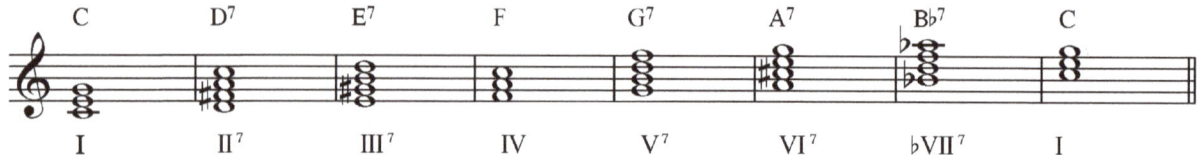

A great idea is to experiment with combinations of this dominant 7 harmony and the more conventional harmony.

Use the following chart to locate the diatonic harmony and common substitutes in all 12 keys:

I	iim/II7	iiim/III7	IV	V/V7	vim/VI7	bVII7	vii dim	I
C	D	E	F	G	A	Bb	B	C
F	G	A	Bb	C	D	Eb	E	F
Bb	C	D	Eb	F	G	Ab	A	Bb
Eb	F	G	Ab	Bb	C	Db	D	Eb
Ab	Bb	C	Db	Eb	F	Gb	G	Ab
Db	Eb	F	Gb	Ab	Bb	Cb	C	Db
Gb	Ab	Bb	Cb	Db	Eb	Fb	F	Gb
F#	G#	A#	B	C#	D#	E	E#	F#
B	C#	D#	E	F#	G#	A	A#	B
E	F#	G#	A	B	C#	D	D#	E
A	B	C#	D	E	F#	G	G#	A
D	E	F#	G	A	B	C	C#	D
G	A	B	C	D	E	F	F#	G

Applying to the Guitar

You have probably realized that some of the chords mentioned in the above harmonies we have not yet covered. By the end of this text you will have learned voicings for all of the chord shapes illustrated above. Some of these chords require harder techniques and we will avoid those chord shapes for now. Let us focus on the shapes we know and use them in the key of C.

In the key of C, the following known shapes can be used at this point:

I	iim/II7	iiim/III7	IV	V/V7	vim/VI7	bVII7	vii dim	I
C Cadd9*	Dm Dsus2* D7	Em E7		G G7	Am A7			C Cadd9

The add9 and sus2 chords change the texture of the sound, but not the harmonic function

The majority of progressions will start on the I chord. This tends to be the easiest way to construct musical chord sequences but is not your only option. A progression can start in another area and work its way to the I chord.

Let us look at our current available chords in the key of G:

I	iim/II7	iiim/III7	IV	V/V7	vim/VI7	bVII7	vii dim	I
G	Am Asus2 A7	B7	C Cadd9	D D7	Em E7			G

Here are the current open chords in the key of D:

I	iim/II7	iiim/III7	IV	V/V7	vim/VI7	bVII7	vii dim	I
D Dsus2	Em E7		G	A Asus2 A7	B7	C C7		D Dsus2

Here are the current options in the key of A:

I	iim/II7	iiim/III7	IV	V/V7	vim/VI7	bVII7	vii dim	I
A Asus2	B7		D Dsus2	E E7		G G7		A Asus2

And the options in the key of E:

I	iim/II7	iiim/III7	IV	V/V7	vim/VI7	bVII7	vii dim	I
E			A Asus2	B7		D D7		E

As of now we have not learned any chords based of **sharps** or **flats** (*accidentals*). As the keys become more accidental heavy, we will have less available options at this point. The keys of C G D A and E are the most commonly used in acoustic guitar composition. These **open chords** (chords combining open and fretted notes) are easier to play and have nice full ringing sounds that support a vocalist very comfortably. They are also very easy to transpose to other keys with the use of a helpful yet inexpensive tool.

The Capo

The capo is a clamping device that shortens the strings making the pitch of each string higher. Think of it as moving the nut of the guitar to a different fret of the neck. The capo will transpose every open chord you play by a distance equal to the fret number. For example, a capo placed on the second fret would transpose all chords up a whole step. Were you to finger a C chord shape with the capo in this position, it would sound as a D chord. The G shape would sound as an A.

Placing the Capo

There are several different types of capos, but a clamping capo with a spring based tightening mechanism is recommended. The capo should depress the strings only enough to eliminate buzzing. If you tighten more than necessary, you will cause intonation issues. Look at how the guitar neck is thinner up towards the nut and gets thicker as it approaches the body. A lighter tension should be used as the capo gets closer to the body.

Capo

When placing the capo make sure it is aligned latitudinally with the fret. Maintaining a bit of space between the capo and the fret will allow for the guitar to stay in tune better.

Correct Capo Placement 👍

INCORRECT Capo Placement 👎👎👎

After placing the capo press down on the 6th, 5th, and 4th strings simultaneously to stretch them out a bit. If possible, retune the guitar with the capo <u>on</u>.

Try the following progression with the capo on the 2nd fret:

Play the shapes as you see them as opposed to trying to figure out the transposition.

The progression will sound as follows:

You might be wondering why the capo is necessary in this situation since you have learned the A, E and D chords in open position. Remove the capo and play the progression:

There should be a noticeable timbre change. One reason for this is the number of strings used in each chord is different. The other reason is that the voicing order has changed. As a songwriter it is important to factor in these considerations which extend beyond just playing the correct chord shapes. Listen to the **voice leading**- how the notes in the chord resolve from one to the next, and decide which best suits your vision for the song.

Another consideration would be matching the key to the optimal range on the vocalist (whether it be you or someone else. Experiment with different capo positions until the vocalist sounds comfortable over all the sections of the song. Sometimes just raising the capo by 1 fret can really make a vocalist shine as they push just a little harder to hit their notes.

Try some of these chord progressions from previous chapters using the following capo placements. At this point you have not learned the note names on every string and every fret so it is not necessary to worry about the exact names of the chords you are playing. We will cover this material in later chapters. Slash mark without stems require you to make up your own rhythms.

Capo 1:

Capo 3:

Capo 4:

Capo 5:

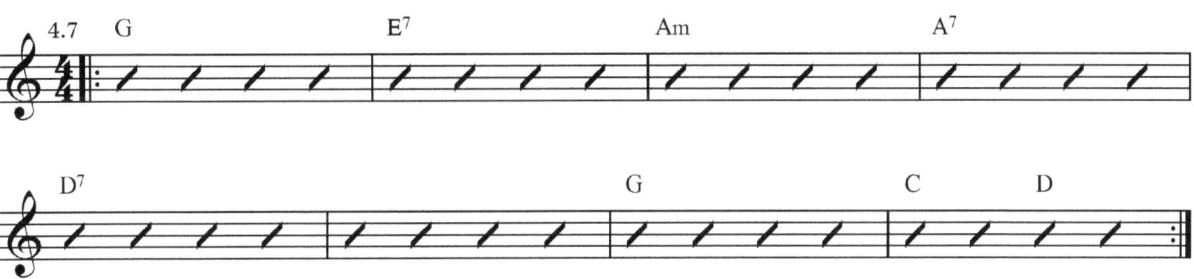

Capo 7:

Interpreting Progressions as Roman Numerals

At this point we are flying 🪰 blindly 😎 in some of the keys once the capo is applied. For now this is ok and will also help you develop a skill that is most helpful to songwriters: conceiving progressions as Roman numerals.

Let us revisit our initial progression:

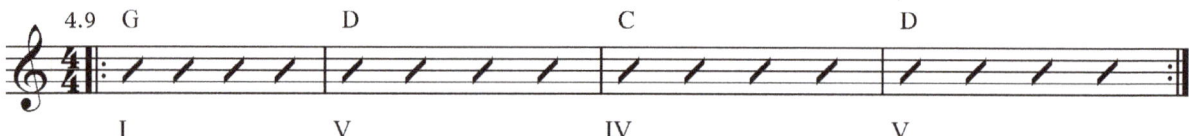

By recognizing the function of each chord, we can easily transpose via capo as all chords would retain their functions in the new keys.

Try interpreting the following chord progressions throughout multiple keys:

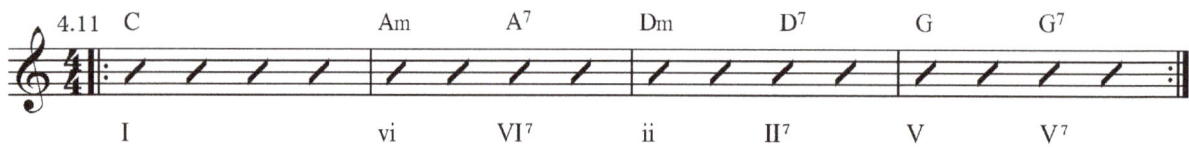

Try these next progressions without a key given. Remember you still have some gaps to fill in as far as complete recognition of diatonic harmony in each key so choose a key that will allow for you to use an open chord shape for each Roman numeral:

The IV in this progression is a dominant 7, which deviates from conventional diatonic harmony. This is to remind you the importance of experimenting with different sounds. Otherwise music would all be the same 😴!

You should be able to find a few different starting points for this progression:

Remember that as a songwriter you will want to let your ear tell you which voicings of the chords sound the best in context of each other. Although at this point you have several ways of navigating the progression above, use your ear to decide the best voice leading and then use a capo if necessary to change the key.

Arpeggiation

An **arpeggio** is a chord in which each note is performed individually, one after the next. This can be a very effective accompaniment tool to give the chords a different texture than would be created by striking all of the notes simultaneously. When using arpeggiation for an accompaniment pattern you will typically let all notes ring out as long as possible. The following examples will assume you will let the notes ring as you pass on to the next.

There are two methods of arpeggiating chords on the guitar with the right hand, pick-style and fingerstyle. We will learn about fingerstyle technique in upcoming chapters.

Arpeggiation with the Pick

Begin by playing a C chord in an ascending arpeggiation. All pick directions should be downstrokes in this example.

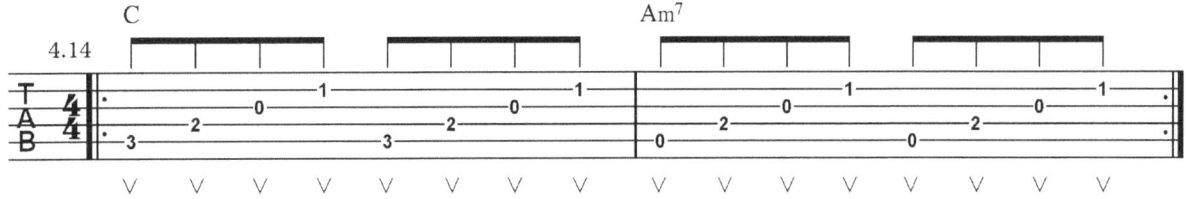

Try the next descending example with all up strokes. Strive for an even sound to each note played.

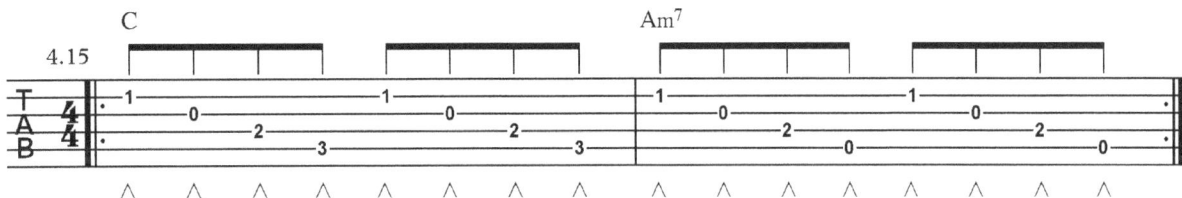

Now combine the two:

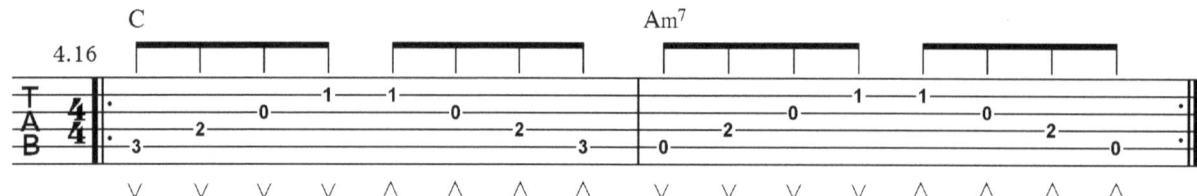

Try to balance the upstroke attacks so they sound as consistent as the downstrokes. The upstroke tends to be harder to execute evenly.

The next exercise will have you practice alternate picking. Once again, even balance and timing should be your main focus:

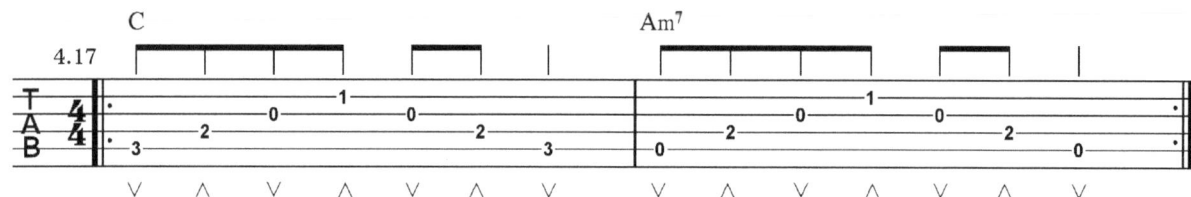

Here is a string skipping exercise. A great way to embellish your progressions is to jump over strings to break up the arpeggio order.

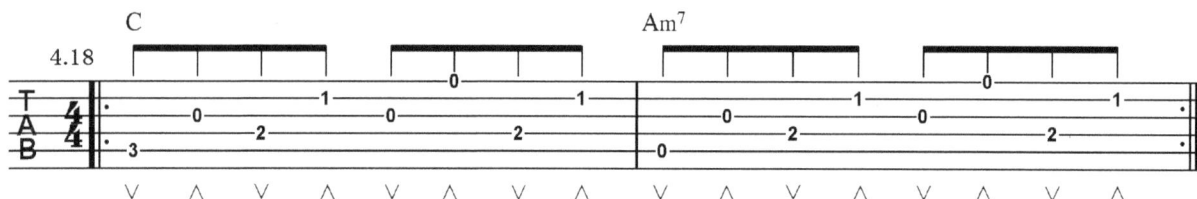

There is a big initial string skip here:

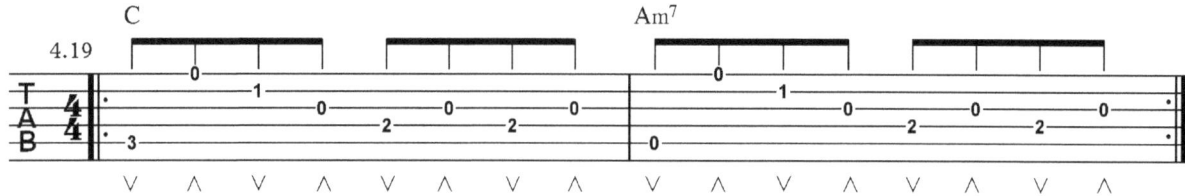

Let's look at a longer progression with varying string groups for each chord.

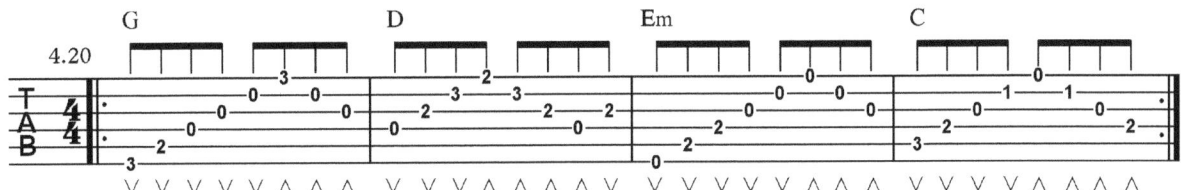

Watch the pick directions here. Try to flow with the direction of the arpeggio, changing directions at the start of the ascent or decent.

Here is the same sequence, but this time use alternate pick directions:

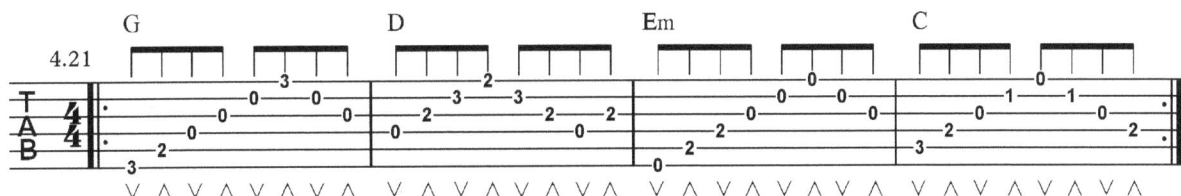

Ideally you will become equally comfortable with each picking option. Until then, chose the one that is easiest for you to execute smoothly.

Chapter 4 Practice Progression Creation:

What we want to do with the information learned in this chapter, is to create accompaniment to a melody. As songwriters we must use the guitar to enhance a melody. Consider the following melody in the key of G:

Play this simple melody to hear what it sounds like. Repeat it a few times to get used to it. Now try to sing the melody. As you sing experiment with different diatonic open chord shapes you know until you find a combination you think really enhances the melody the best. Here is one example (and keep in mind there could be many good combinations):

Strum these chords in whole and/or half note values so you can hear the harmony working against the melody. Now we will add arpeggiation to the accompaniment part.

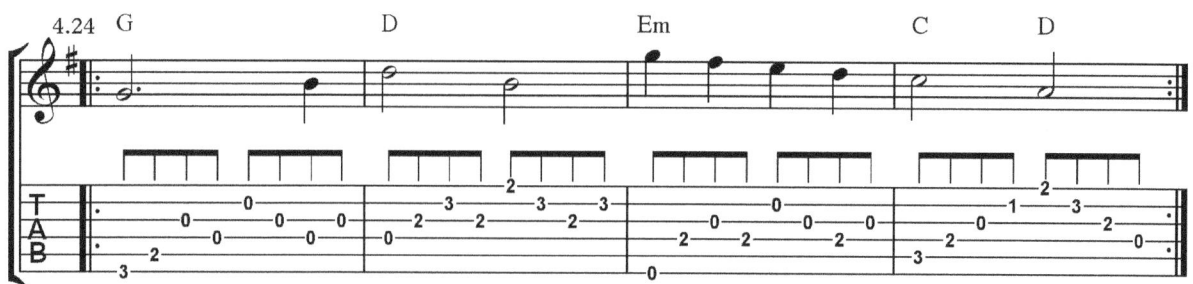

Now it's your turn. Add your own diatonic chords to the melody, followed by an arpeggiated accompaniment pattern:

The final step will be transposition. Using a capo find the best key for you to sing the melody. Transpose the exercise to best fit your vocal range.

Try creating more melodies (and even lyrics if you want), accompaniment progressions and arpeggiation patterns through the same process. You could also try starting with the accompaniment part first and constructing a melody on top of it.

Once you get comfortable with diatonic harmony, experiment with all open chord shapes to see if you can produce some interesting progressions. Remember, diatonic harmony can be very helpful in crafting songs but you should also look for clever ways to use some sounds outside of this conventional approach.

Chapter 5: Meter, Triplets and Alternating Bass

Time Signatures

Up to this point, all the examples given have been in 4/4 or "common" time. It is important to be aware of what the time signatures mean.

 Beats per measure

 Type of note receiving one beat/count

In 4/4 time, there will be four quarter notes counted per measure.

Let us now try some chord strumming examples in 3/4 time. Simply count to three instead of 4.

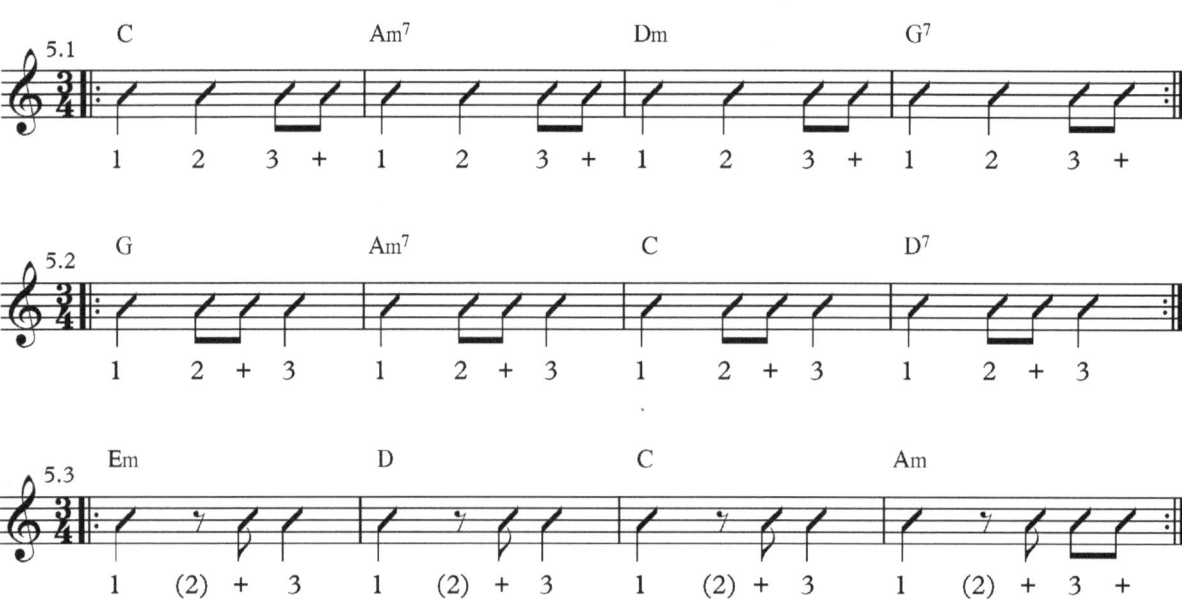

Dotted notes

We encountered a dotted quarter note in an early example in chapter 3 but have not seen any in our chord progression exercises thus far. This concept can be tricky at first. The dot adds half the value to the rhythm.

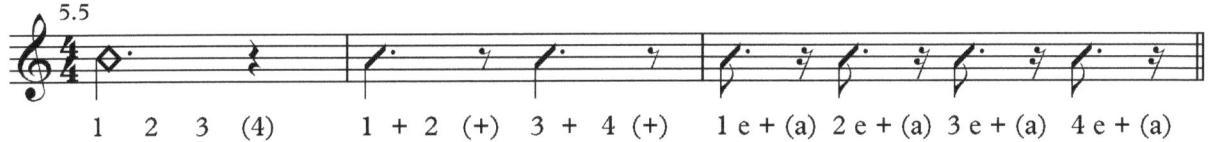

The dotted half note holds for three beats, the dotted eighth for one and a half beats, and so on.

You can also see dotted notes placed off the beat:

You will commonly find dotted notes followed or preceded by the leftover note values:

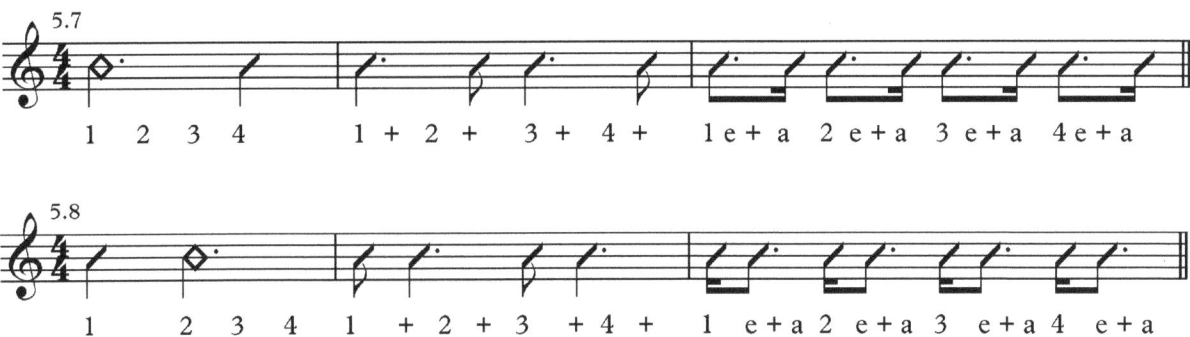

When strumming dotted values smaller than a dotted half note, it is <u>EXTREMELY</u> important to keep the flow of your right hand moving in a down-up direction. Remove the pick from the strings when the attack is not necessary and keep the wrist moving in the air.

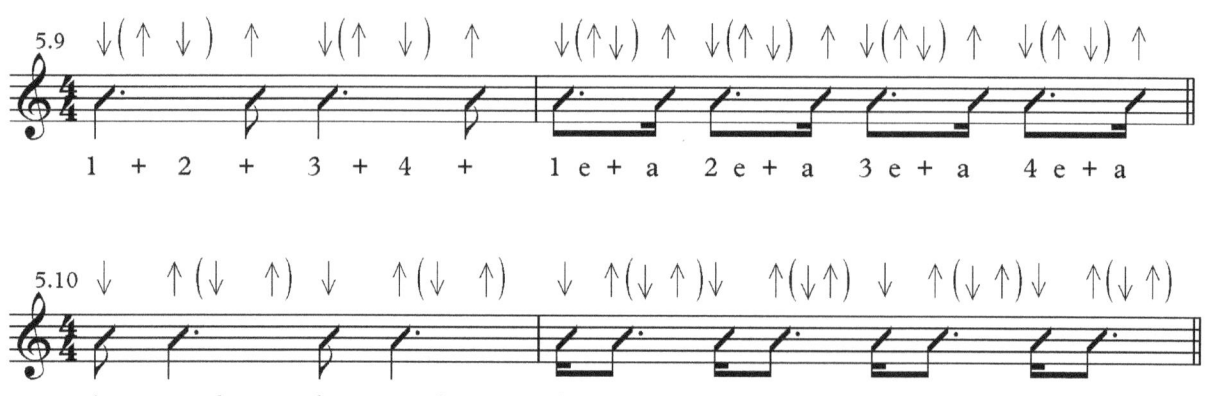

Try playing the following chord progressions featuring dotted rhythms:

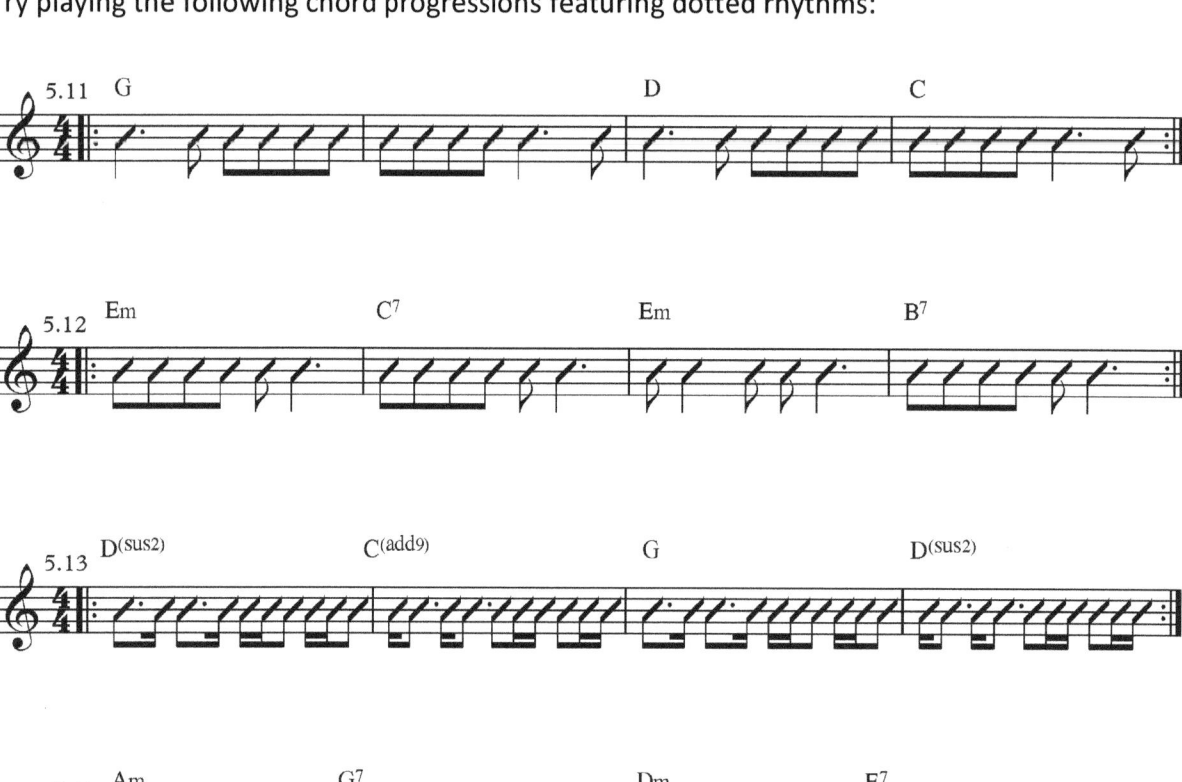

Meter

When the denominator changes (the bottom value), the concept of how the time is felt also changes. In time signatures with a quarter note denominator, there are potentially different emphases placed on each beat. In 4/4 time the measure is interpreted as divided in half. This is known as **duple meter**. The same is true for a meter not yet encountered in this text: 2/4.

3/4 time is considered **triple meter**. This would pertain to any meter in which the count is divisible by 3.

Meter can also be classified by **subdivision** a term referring to how each beat is broken into a smaller, yet consistent, pulse. **Simple meter** suggests that the bar divides naturally into two equal portions whereas **compound meter** would find the measure broken into three equal segments.

6/8 Time

6/8 technically refers to 6 beats per measure, with the eighth note receiving a count. Interpreting the feel in this manner should be avoided. 6/8 time should break down into two dotted quarter notes:

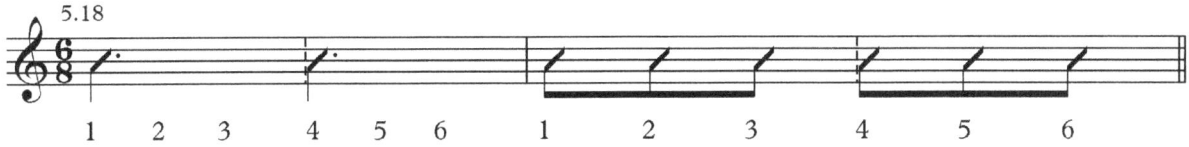

Notice how the dashed line separates the measure between beats 3 and 4. The emphasis of 6/8 should be felt on beat 1 and beat 4. **1**-2-3-**4**-5-6.

A written quarter note in 6/8 time would receive two counts ala a half note in 4/4 or 3/4 time. The beat emphasis would still remain on beats 1 and 4 of your count. A 16th note in 6/8 time would be counted with an "+" similar how the eighth note was counted in 4/4 and 3/4 time.

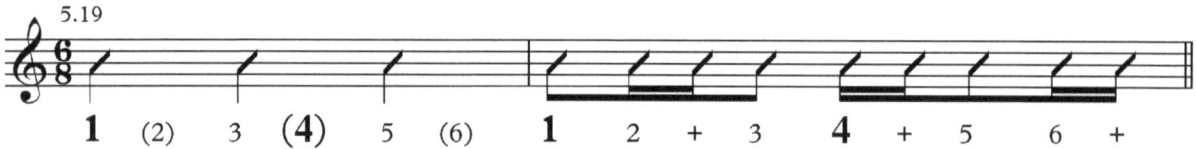

Try out some progressions in 6/8:

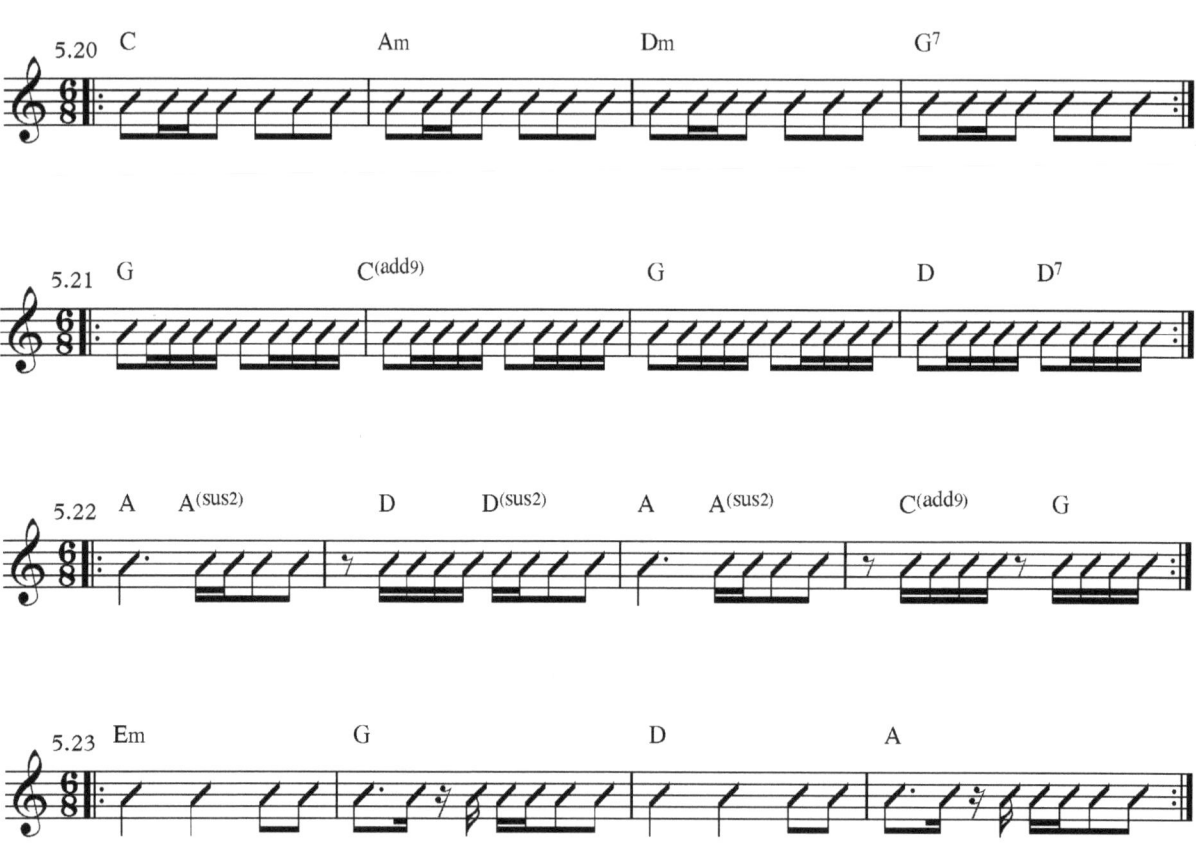

Triplets

Triplets are groups of three notes spaced evenly across the space of two. The best way to understand the triplet is to compare a measure of 6/8 to how the same figure would be written in 4/4:

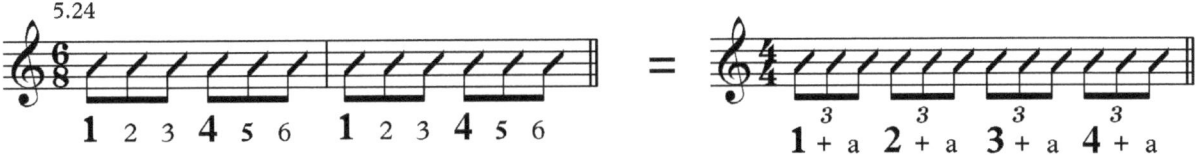

These measures would feel the same. The difference would be that in 6/8 this 'feel' of three subdivisions per emphasized beat would remain constant, whereas in 4/4, the eighth note triplet would not be the primary subdivision of the measure (which would still be eighth and sixteenth notes). The triplet feel has a sort of rhythmic tug against the actual note value.

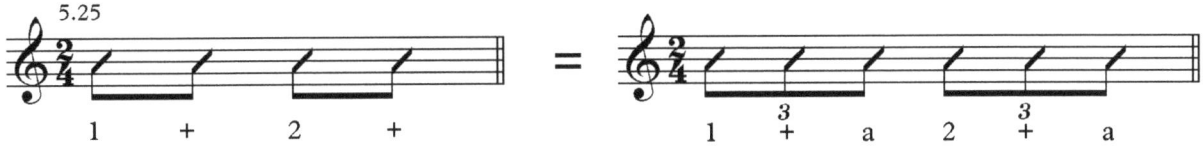

Notice these measures in 2/4 time (only 2 beats per measure here) would last the same duration. The '+' of the triplet would happen earlier in time than the '+' of the eighth note. The 'a' of the triplet would occur a bit later in time than the '+' of the eighth note.

For further clarification examine how these two rhythms would be played the same (although the 4/4 side would be considered as a slower tempo):

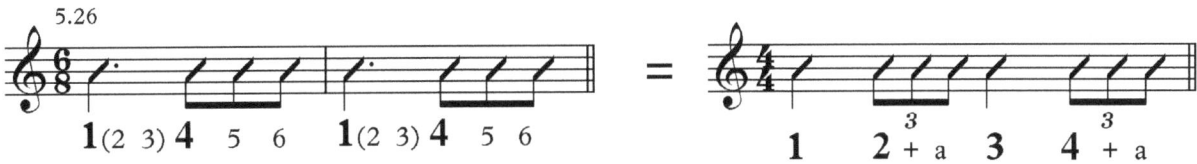

Pick Direction for Triplet Rhythms

When performing triplets you have two picking options:

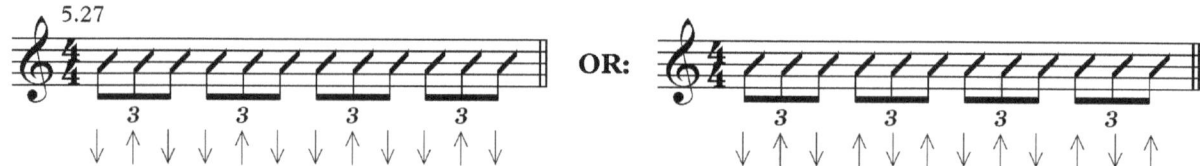

In the first figure, the down pick resets on each downbeat. This is advantageous because it will not affect the method of strumming we have learned up to this point. This makes it easier to go back to eighth and sixteenth note rhythms from a triplet figure.

The second figure is an alternate picking approach that will reverse the picking on beats 2 and 4. I suggest using this rhythm when you have a continuous stream of triplets or when you are encountering extremely fast tempos.

Try some triplet-based progressions and experiment with your pick directions:

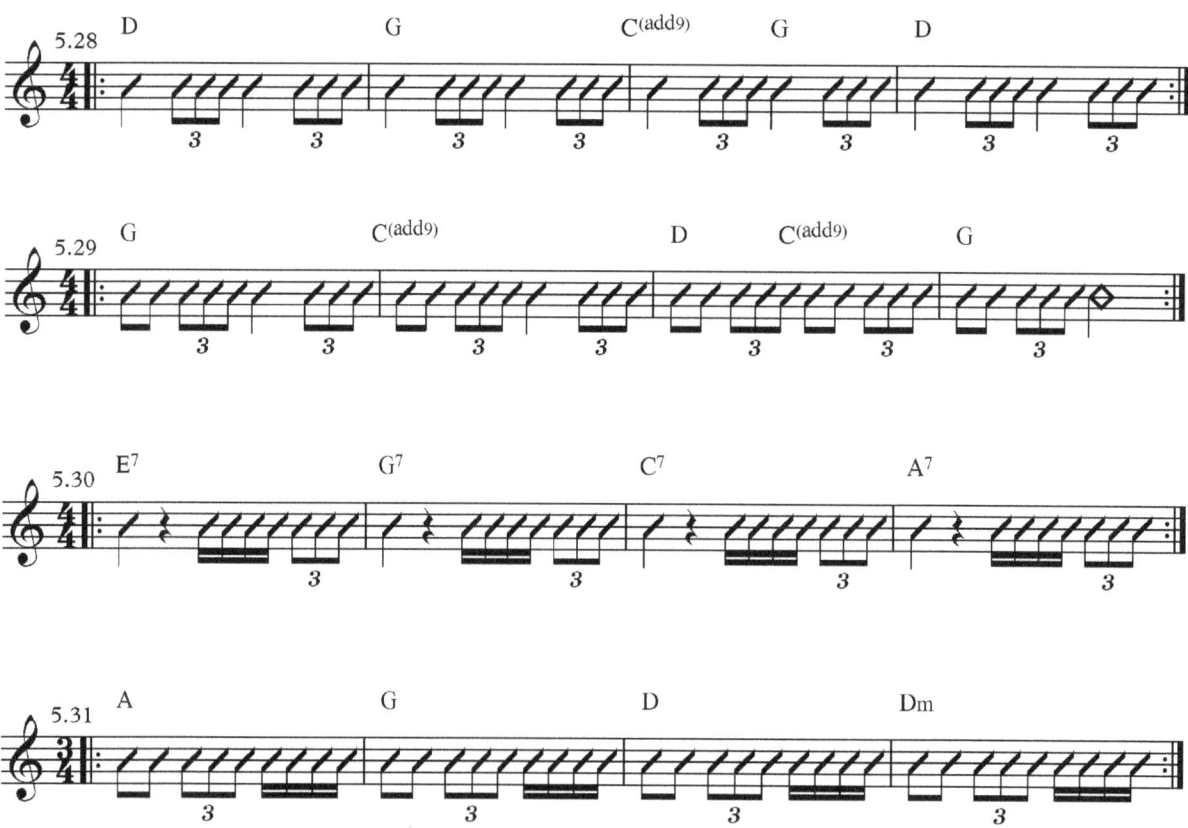

Asus4:

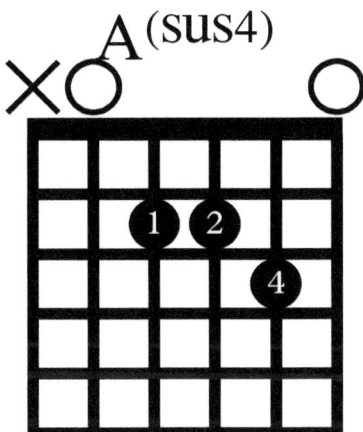

1. Place the first finger on the second fret of the 4th string
2. Place the second finger behind it on the second fret of the 3rd string
3. Place the fourth finger behind it on the third fret of the 2nd string
4. Pluck each string from the 5th to the 1st, one at a time to make sure all pitches sound
5. Remember to avoid the 6th string in this chord

Or:

1. Play an A
2. Place the fourth finger one fret ABOVE the third finger on the 2nd string
3. Pluck each string from the 5th to the 1st, one at a time to make sure all pitches sound
4. Remember to avoid the 6th string in this chord

Songwriting Tip: The Asus4 is often used as an embellishment to the A chord.

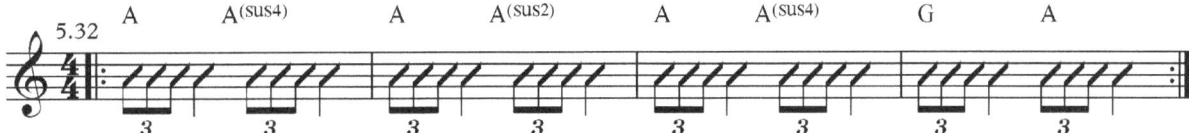

Dsus4:

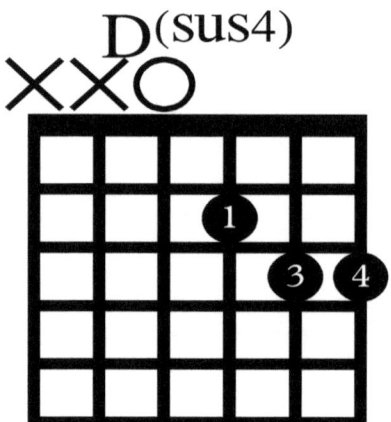

1. Place the first finger on the second fret of the 3rd string
2. Place the third finger behind it on the third fret of the 2nd string
3. Place the fourth finger behind it on the third fret of the 1st string
4. Pluck each string from the 4th string to the 1st string
5. Avoid the 6th and 5th strings in this chord

Or:

1. Play a D chord
2. Place the fourth finger one fret ABOVE the second finger on the 1st string
3. Pluck each string from the 4th string to the 1st
4. Avoid the 6th and 5th strings

Songwriting Tip: The Dsus4 is often used as an embellishment to the D chord.

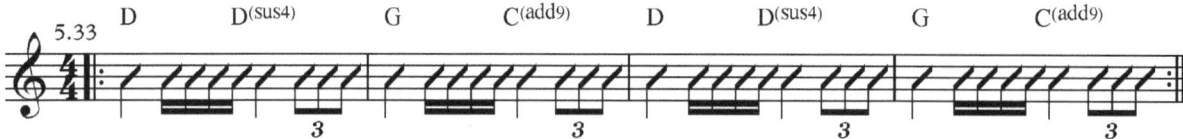

Esus4:

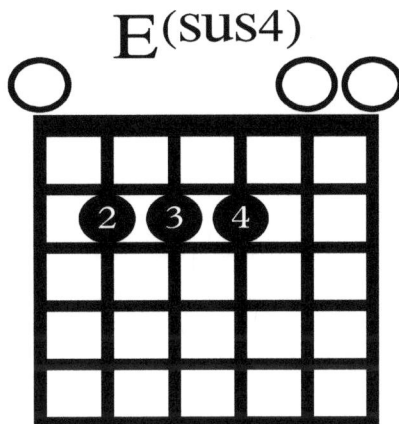

1. Place the second finger on the second fret of the 5th string
2. Place the third finger behind it on the second fret of the 4th string
3. Place the fourth finger behind it on the second fret of the 3rd string

Or:

1. Play an E chord
2. Place the fourth finger on fret ABOVE the first finger on the 3rd string

Songwriting Tip: *The Esus4 is often used as an embellishment to the E chord.*

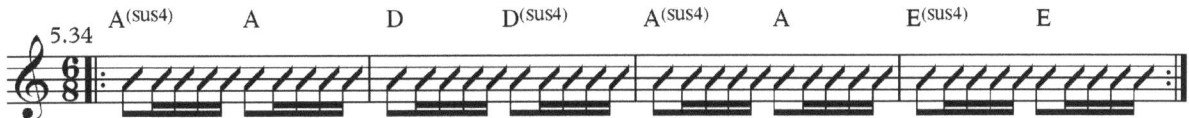

Alternating Bass Note Accompaniment

One way to get more mileage out of your open chord shapes is to use alternating bass note accompaniment. This process separates your chords into two registers, bass notes and upper voices. Try this example to get started:

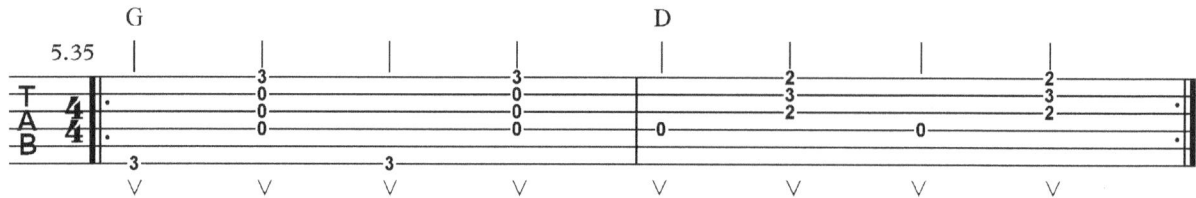

Notice how on the G chord we are completely skipping the 5th string. This is intentional so as to create more separation of the ranges. Since we are working with two fewer strings on the D, we will play all four.

Next, we will move our bass note down from a root to a fifth. Try this on a C chord:

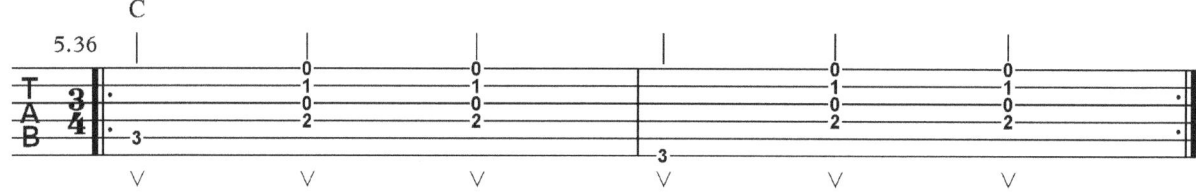

Move your third finger back and forth between the 5th and 6th strings respectively in this exercise. When playing the bass note on the 6th string, lean the third finger over just enough to mute the 5th string. This will allow you to not have to worry about absolute precision with your picking hand, which should allow for a more comfortable feel.

Which string should you alternate to?

As I mentioned earlier you are moving a root to a fifth as far as scale degrees go. However, you don't need to know much music theory to use this technique. If the chord's lowest note starts on the 5th or 4th string, all you need to do is alternate to the bass note directly ACROSS and over from your lowest pitch:

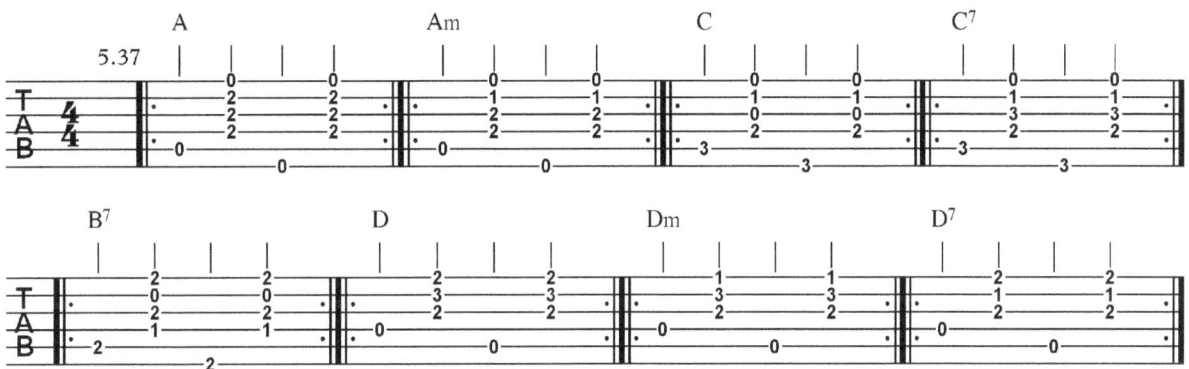

Apply this method to any other chord shapes you know, rooted off the 5th or 4th strings.

On the 6th string, the process is not as cut and dry. You need to alternate UP a fifth in this case. Fortunately, there are only a few chords you have learned on the 6th string thus far; The E family and the G family. Here is the way to treat alternating bass notes off these two chord families:

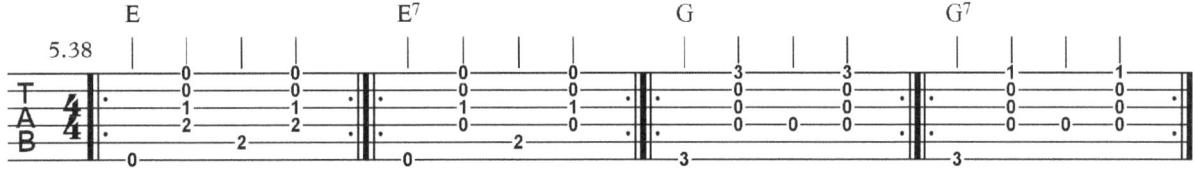

Remember to avoid the 5th string in until beat 3. The sound will get very muddy if you use the 5th string in conjunction with the remaining chord tones.

Chapter 5 Practice Progressions:

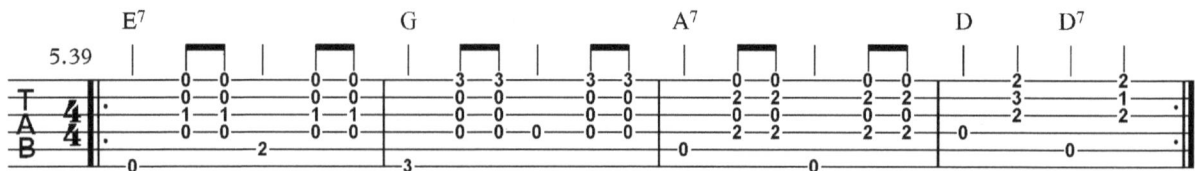

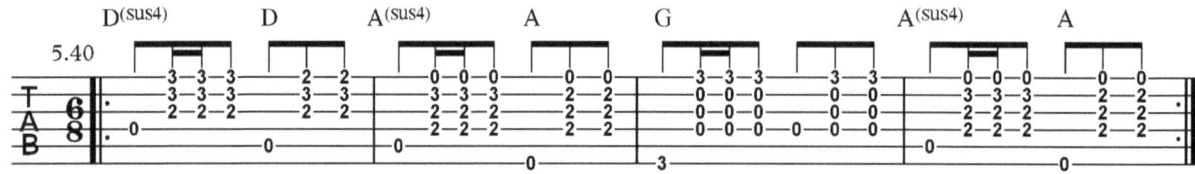

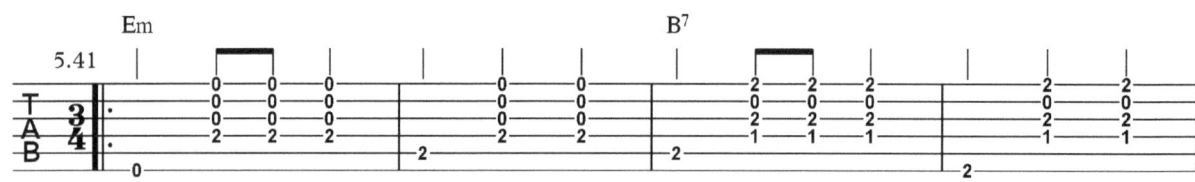

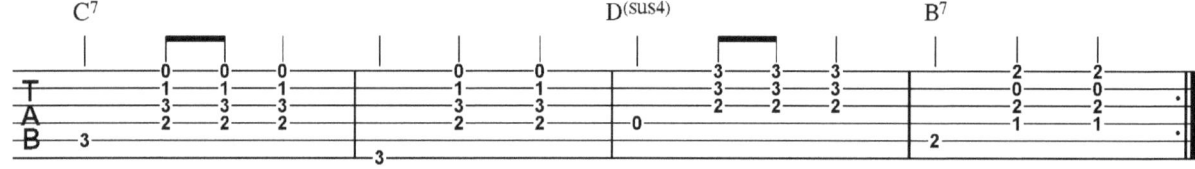

Chapter 6: Introduction to Barre Chords and Fingerstyle

Barring

The barre chord is the most dreaded chord shape for the novice guitar player. The term **barre** refers to multiple strings being pressed down by the *same* finger. This will require more finger strength than any chord shapes you have played so far. There is also a little bit of strategy involved as well.

Being able to barre effectively requires a lot of practice, which will help you to develop muscle 💪. But equally important are the angles involved.

Look at your index finger on the left hand. With your palm facing you, run your right index finger along your left. Notice the grooves?

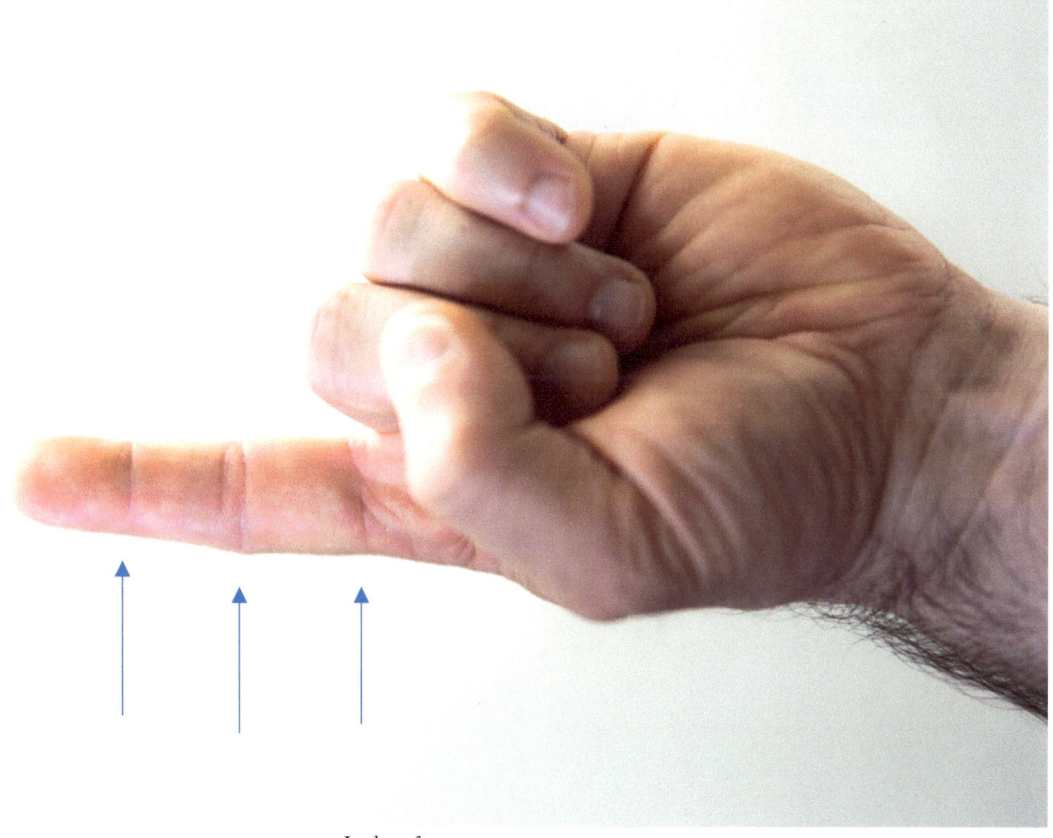

Index finger grooves

These grooves create an unevenness across the finger. If you were to try to press down multiple strings with this same finger, some of the strings might be in the grooves, making them far more difficult to press down. With your thumb facing the sky run your right index finger along the side of your left index finger.

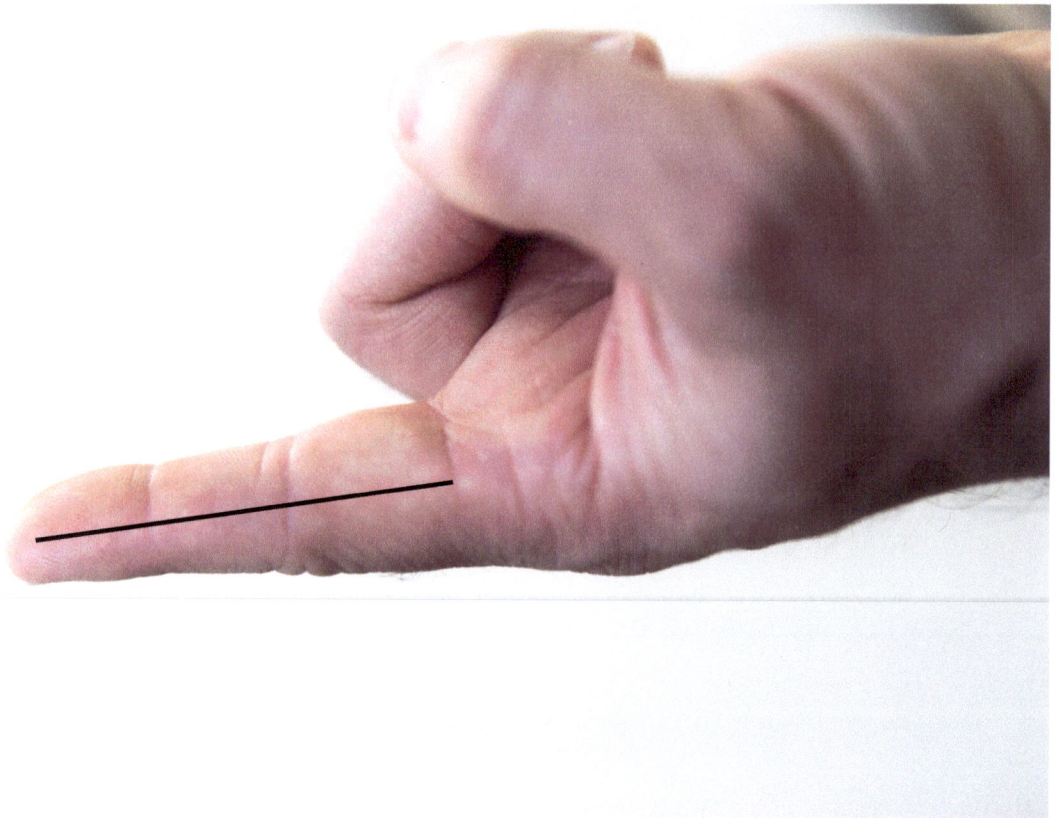

Index finger side shot

Other than a slightly protruding knuckle bone, this should feel like a far more even surface. <u>This side of your finger is the key to barring.</u> If you angle your finger backwards towards the direction of the guitar nut, you will be able to accomplish successful barring much faster. More strength will still need to be developed of course, but this should help you reach you barring goals much faster. You do not have to over exaggerate this angle, just enough so that the flatter part of your index finger is pressing down on the desired barre.

F (basic):

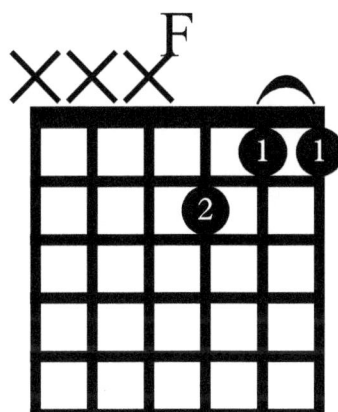

1. Barre the first finger across the first fret of BOTH the 1st and 2nd strings
2. Make sure both strings sound before proceeding further
3. Place the second finger on the second fret of the 3rd string
4. Pluck each string from the 3rd to the 1st, one at a time to make sure all pitches sound
5. Remember to avoid the 6th 5th and 4th strings in this chord

Troubleshooting the F chord:

-Is your first finger angled backwards so as to be pressing on the flattest surface?
-Is the angle of your first finger shifting in the wrong direction when you add your second finger?
-Are you using proper thumb placement on the back of the neck to allow the thumb to apply the most pressure?
-Are you squeezing hard enough?

Rather than putting this chord in a progression at this point, my recommendation is once you form the chord and get it sounding consistently clear in each string, take your fingers off the neck (leaving the thumb in place), and then reform the chord. Do this over and over to increase strength and accuracy.

Dm7

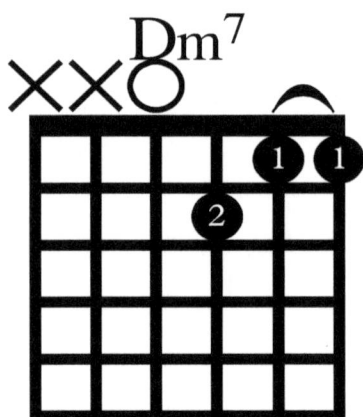

1. Barre the first finger across the first fret of BOTH the 1st and 2nd strings
2. Make sure both strings sound before proceeding further
3. Place the second finger on the second fret of the 3rd string
4. Pluck each string from the 4th to the 1st, one at a time to make sure all pitches sound
5. Remember to avoid the 6th and 5th strings in this chord

Or:

1. Play a F(basic)
2. Pluck each string from the 4th to the 1st one at a time to make sure all pitches sound
3. Remember to avoid the 6th and 5th strings in this chord

Try this simple progression to get started. Remember to focus on use the correct amount of strings in each chord:

Upstrokes on the F (basic) chord:

Right now it may be difficult to perform upwards strums on the F chord as doing will most likely cause you to play the open 4th string (resulting in a Dm7). A trick is to edge the fleshy tip of your second finger over to slightly touch the 4th string which should mute the string. This way if you pick happens to hit the 4th string in the process of the strum you will still only be hearing the three desired pitches of the F (basic) chord.

Try this progression to practice this muting technique:

Movable Chord Shapes

Up to this point, we have not encountered any chord shapes that were movable without the use of a capo. If you think back to the mechanics of the capo you may remember that the capo in essence changed the length of the string and therefore transposed the open chord shapes to a new key. Barre chords follow the exact same principle. Whenever you use a barre chord you are in effect transposing and open chord shape to a different key (this will make more sense once you learn the full barre chord shapes in chapter 8).

For now, the only movable chord shape you know is the F (basic). Moving this chord up from the first fret to the third fret would produce a G chord. Move up two frets from there to get an A chord.

Now why would you need to use this method when you already know a much more full-sounding open G and A chord? Due to the guitar's tuning, you will not find many ways to comfortable play chords such as A flat or F sharp major. Remember that there are pitches in between (sharps and flats) each natural note. So movable chords allow you to find chords in different keys you have yet to see in this book. These concepts will be expanded upon in later chapters as you learn more barre chord shapes.

Another benefit to movable chord shapes is the possibility of arranging chords due to timbre and area of playability. Open chords have a much more distinct ringing quality to their sound and sometimes it may be best if all chords share a similar characteristic. Movable chords might also not need to be re-fingered to slide from one to the other which could produce faster switches when desired.

Bear these concepts in mind as you learn more chords which do not contain any open strings. It may not be completely clear now, but in time understanding these concepts will help your arrangements significantly.

Pick playing vs. Fingerstyle

At this point you've learned how to use a pick. You've been able to strum chords, pluck out arpeggios, and alternate bass note accompaniment. This have given you a very versatile approach to creating rhythm parts for your songs. So...what is fingerstyle guitar and why should you learn it?

As the name implies, fingerstyle guitar is the practice of plucking the strings with your fingers only, no pick in hand. The benefits of this include: the ability to simultaneously strike two pitches on non-adjacent strings, greater control of arpeggiation, and the prospect of separating chords into more distinct parts (bass, melody and middle voices).

You can still strum chords without your pick, albeit with a greater degree of difficulty. But the main focus of fingerstyle playing will be to execute fingering patters not conveniently played with a pick.

The Right Hand

The labeling system for the right hand fingers comes from classical Spanish style guitar.

Thumb = *Pulgar* = *p*
Index = *Indice* = *i*
Middle = *Medio* = *m*
Ring = *Anular* = *a*
Pinky = *Mignolo* = *c (also may be called s or e)*

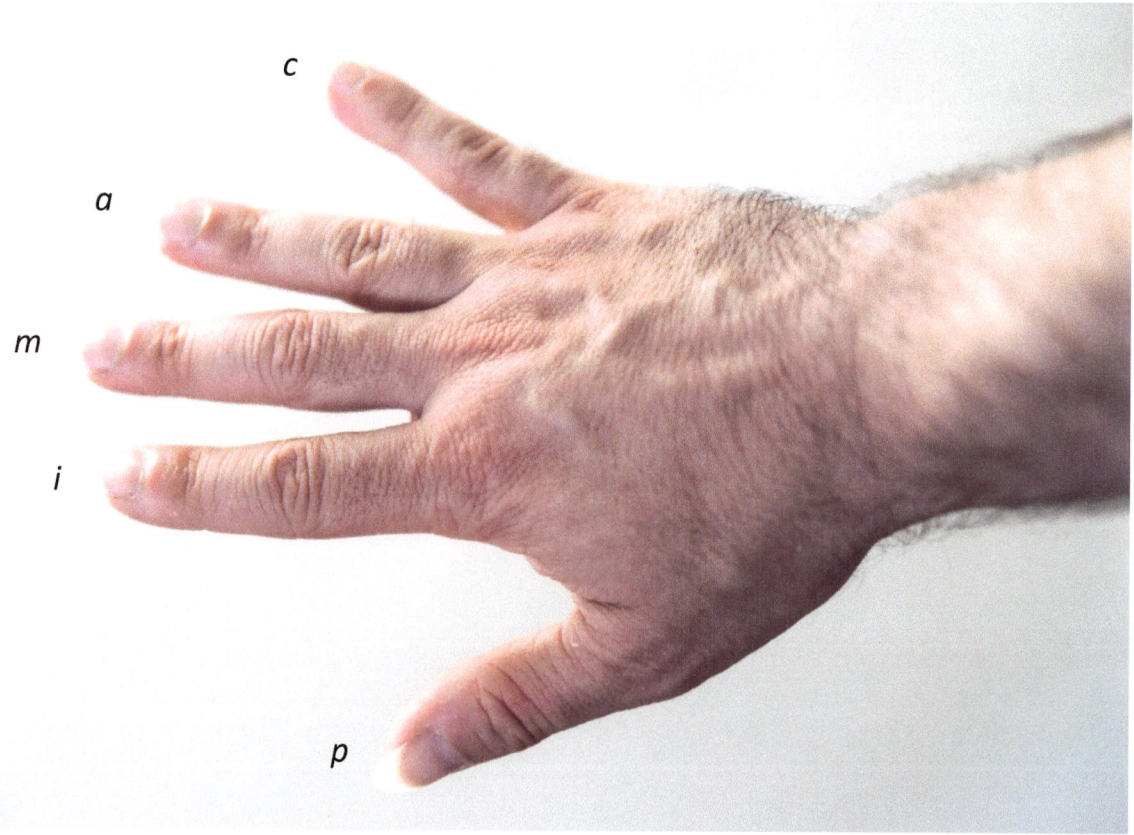

The pinky is rarely used in right hand technique. Exceptions would include a roll across five strings of the guitar.

Here are the typical uses for each finger:

- **The thumb (*p*)** is used *predominantly* on **6th and 5th strings**. Its motion will only pluck downwards on the string. It can sometimes be used to support on the 4th string, if only the highest few strings are being played.
- **The index (*i*)** is commonly used to pluck the **4th string but is not limited to any one string in particular. In ascending patterns it is typically used after the thumb.** The index finger pulls up on the string, opposite from the direction of the thumb.
- **The middle (*m*)** is used in combination with the other fingers in a pattern. It will usually end up plucking the 3rd or second string of the guitar. You can also use it to point at the guitar when you are angry at it 👆. The middle finger pulls up on the string in the same fashion as the index.
- **The ring (*a*) finger is typically used to pluck the highest note in your pattern which would often reside** on the 2nd or 1st string. The ring finger will also pluck upwards on the string.
- **The pinky (*c*) is used only on patterns with 5 to 6 strings in them. Use it as a last resort when there are no other comfortable ways to execute a pattern.**

Right Hand Technique

To begin, extend your right arm out away from your body. Let your hand drop in is most relaxed manner so you are neither using muscles to push it down or hold it up.

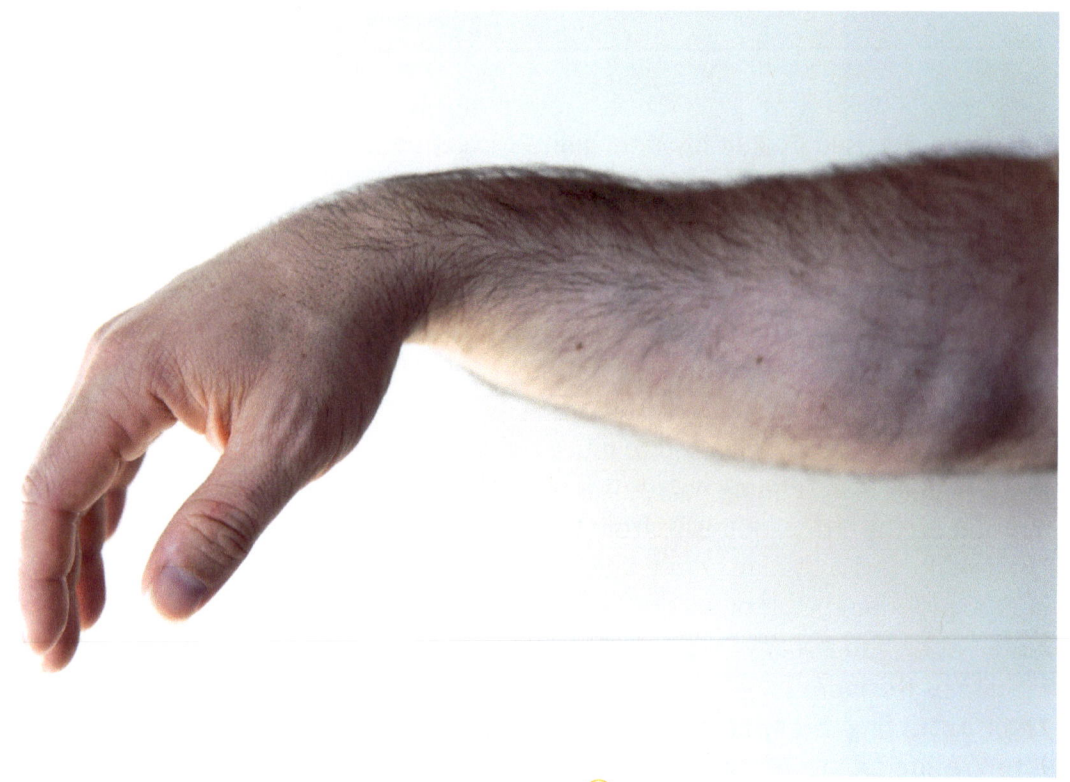

Relaxed right hand 😌

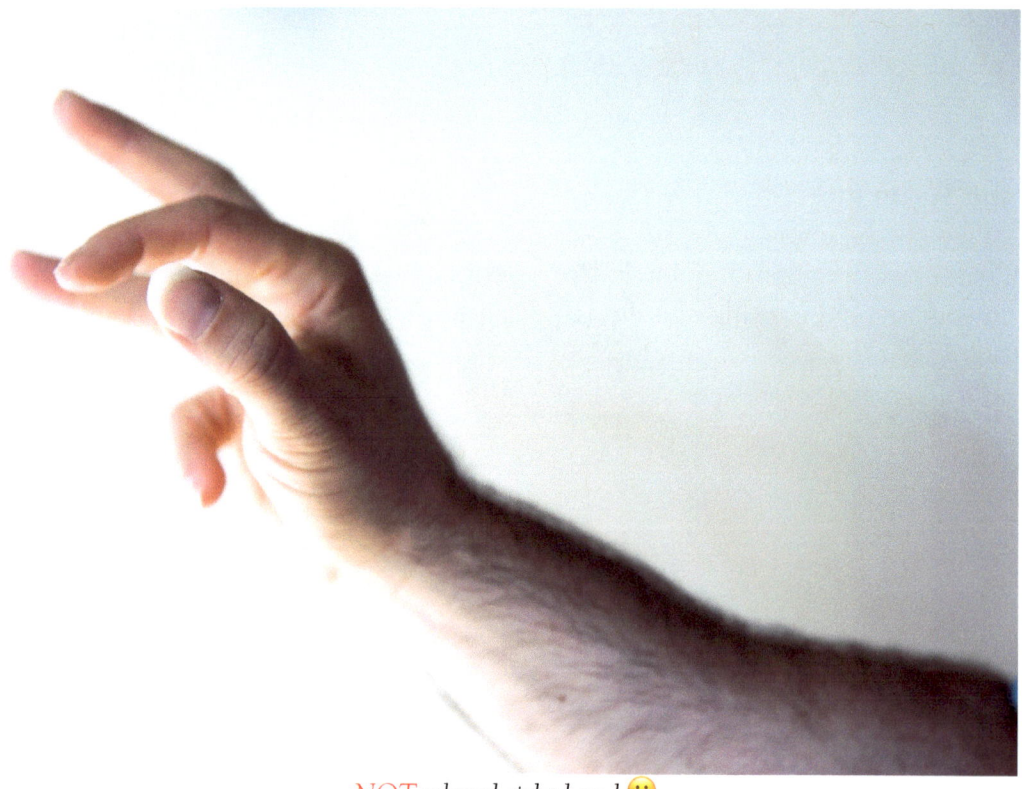

NOT relaxed right hand 😬

While maintaining the angle, bring your arm into the guitar resting your thumb on the 6th string, your index finger on the 3rd string, middle finger on the 2nd string, and ring finger on the 1st string. Keep a nice arch to your wrist, and your fingers extended, but not flayed open.

Right hand placement on strings- front view

Right hand placement on strings- side view

Wrong placement 😒

Make sure to keep the thumb extended higher than the rest of the fingers. Since the thumb will be moving in the opposite direction of the other fingers, this extension is important to avoid collisions, as the other fingers probably don't even have insurance.

Underneath view of correct right hand placement

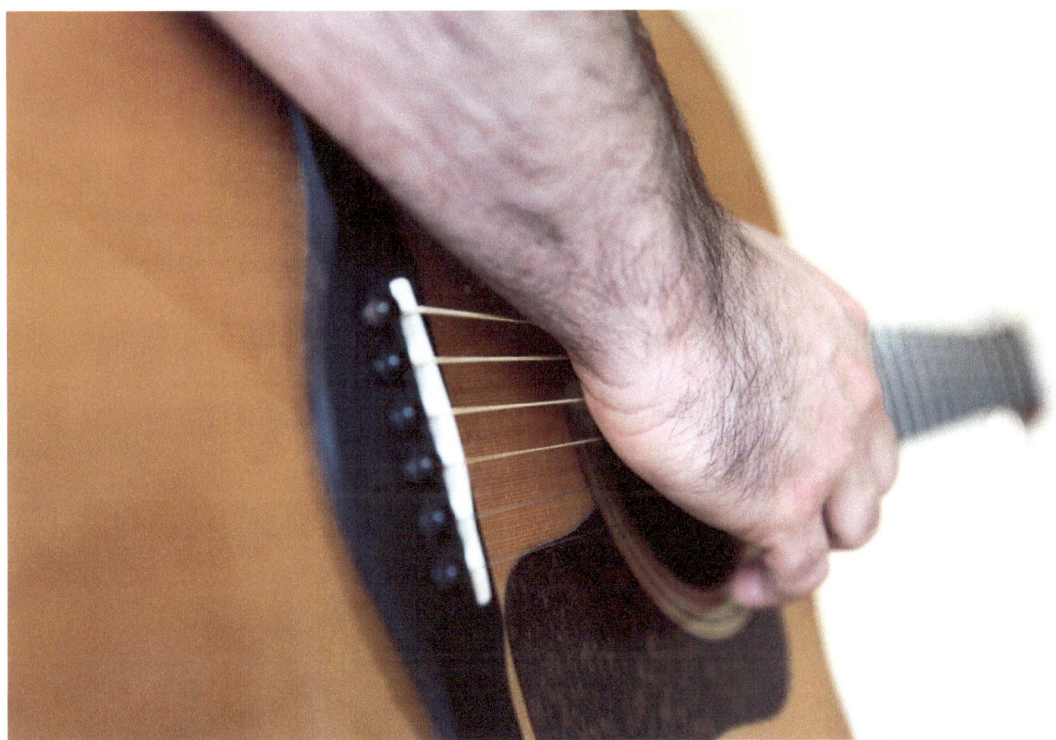

Underneath view of incorrect right hand placement 🚫

The <u>MOST IMPORTANT</u> part of the process is that the fingers are completely *RELAXED* 😎. Keep them loose and even try pushing against them as you plant on the string making sure they aren't stiff. Tension in your fingers will cause uneven playing and will slow you down. You will have to keep reminding yourself to do this as natural instinct usually work against this concept. Go slow and be patient so that this becomes inherent.

The Follow-through

Now that your fingers are placed on the strings it is time to pluck. When you pluck the string concentrate on generating the motion from the top knuckle that connects your finger to your hand. This will be the case for the *i,m,a,* and *e/s* fingers.

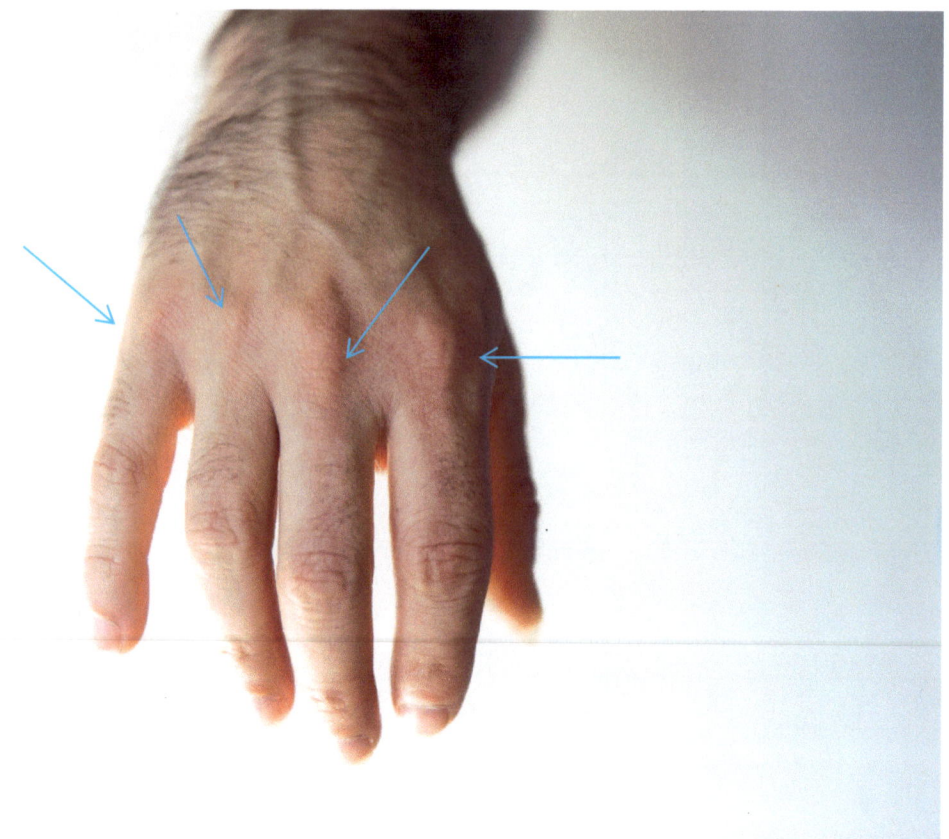

The proper knuckle to activate your motion

Your tendency will probably be to want to pluck from a lower finger joint but you must resist 👊. The follow-through should have enough trajectory to be touching your palm if you were to continue its motion. You will want to maintain full independence of each finger.

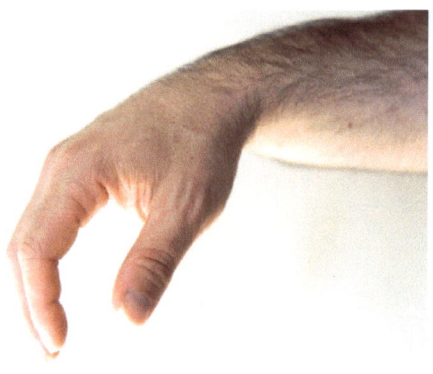

Follow-through starting point no guitar

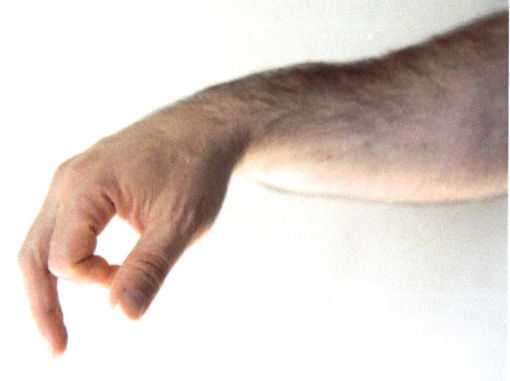

Follow-through ending point no guitar

Follow-through starting point on guitar   *Follow-through ending point on guitar*

The thumb follow-through is similar but will hit the string at a much different angle than the others.

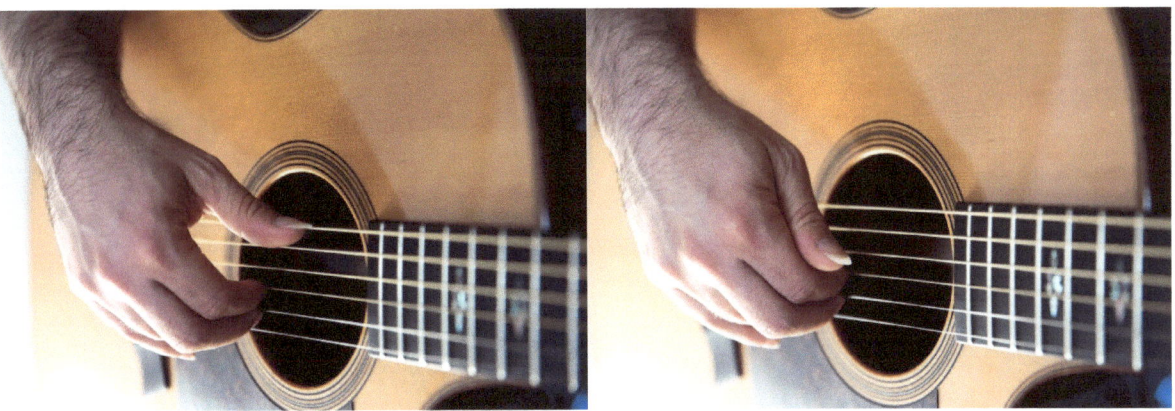

Thumb starting point on guitar   *Thumb ending point on guitar*

Practice plucking each individual string <u>without</u> removing the placement of the other fingers. This is known as a **rest stroke**:

Rest stroke with middle finger starting point   *Rest stroke with middle finger ending point*

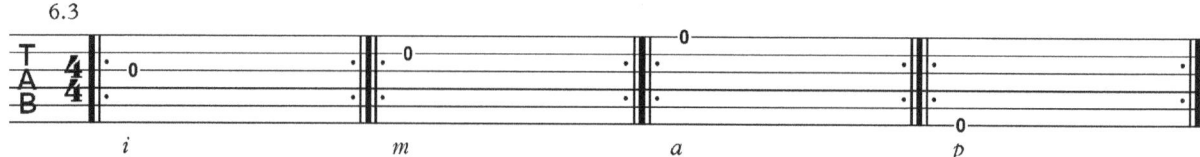

Play each string slowly with the indicated finger. Repeat over and over making sure your position and follow-through are following all of the established guidelines. Don't forget to relax!

Now try alternating between the thumb and the rest of the fingers while holding a G chord:

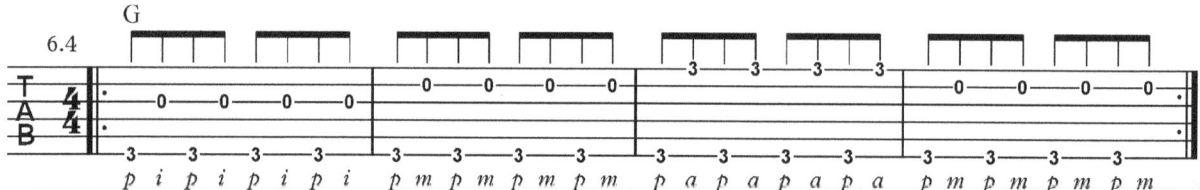

Here is a similar exercise, but this time position your *i, m* and *a* fingers on the 4th, 3rd, and 2nd strings respectively.

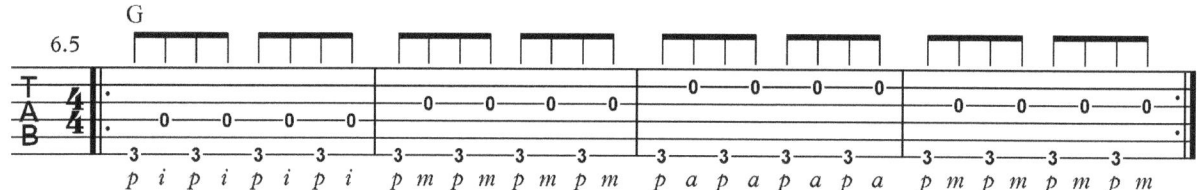

In the next example, the thumb will move in between the 6th string and the 5th string:

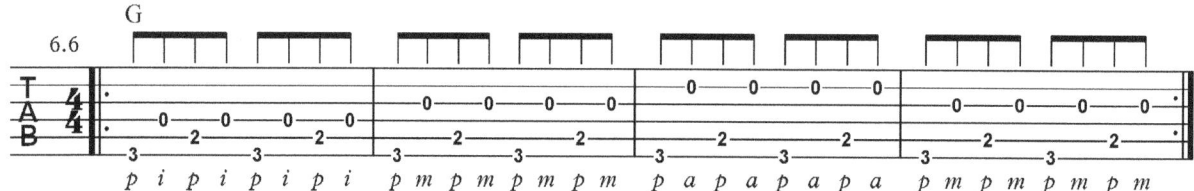

Now we will use string pairs. Make sure both notes are activating simultaneously (relaxing can help this):

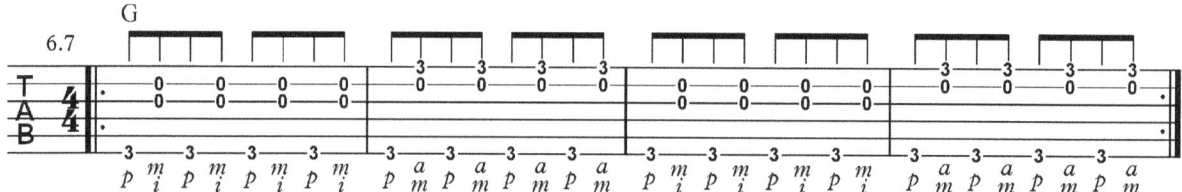

Moving to a C and Amin7 chord now, practice using more fingers in the same measure:

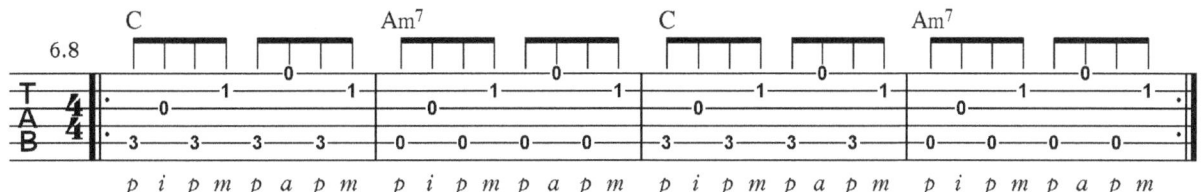

Try the exercise in a different order:

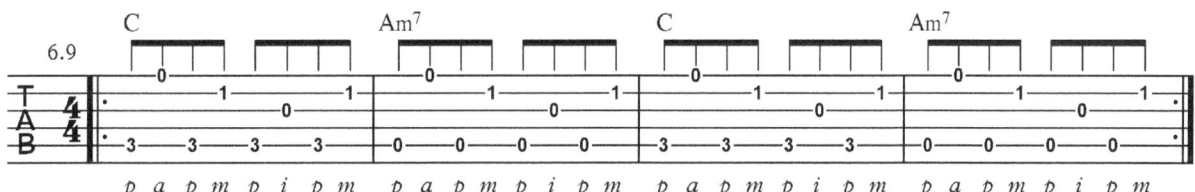

Try alternating the bass notes from 5th to 6th string, similar to what we did in the last chapter:

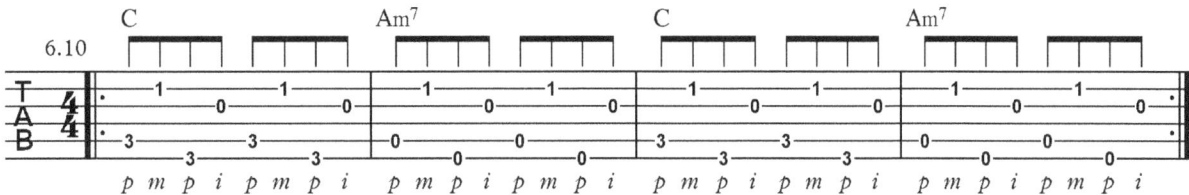

Chapter 6 Practice Progressions:

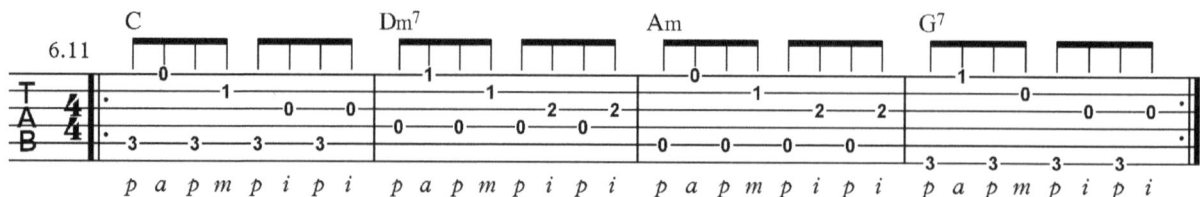

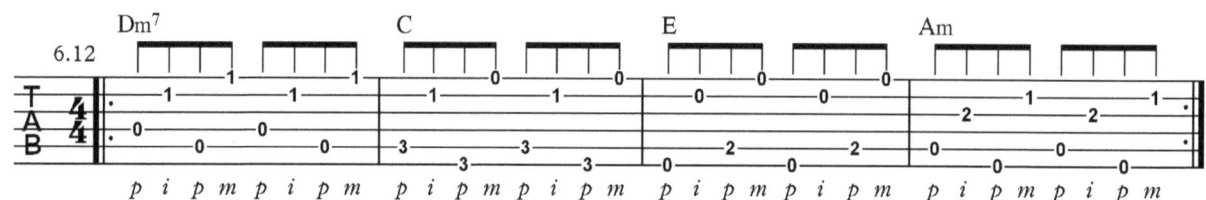

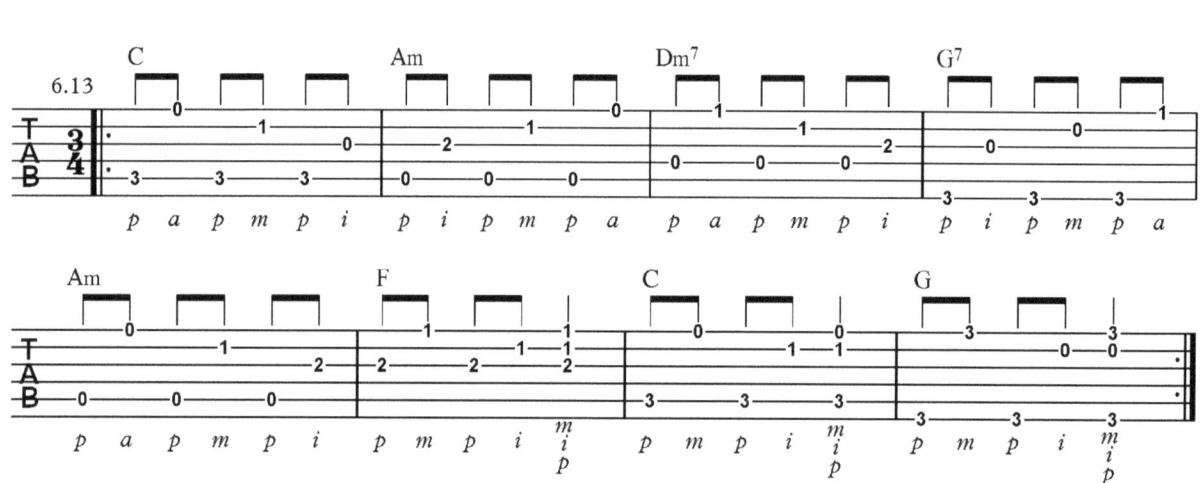

Chapter 7: Barre Chords and Fingerstyle Continued

In this chapter we will learn barre chords containing four strings.

F (Four Strings):

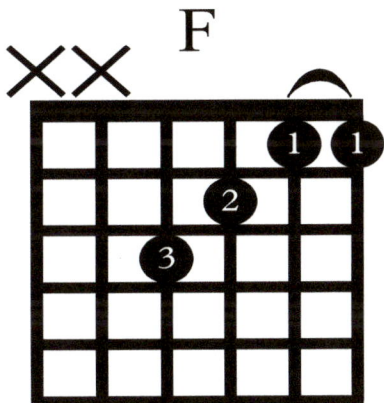

1. Barre the first finger across the first fret of BOTH the 1st and 2nd strings
2. Make sure both strings sound before proceeding further
3. Place the second finger on the second fret of the 3rd string
4. Place the third finger on the third fret of the 4th string
5. Pluck each string from the 1st to the 4th, one at a time to make sure all pitches sound
6. Remember to avoid the 5th and 6th strings in this chord

Troubleshooting the F chord:

-Is your first finger angled backwards so as to be pressing on the flattest surface?
-Is the angle of your first finger shifting in the wrong direction when you add your second finger?
-Are any of the established angles being compromised when you add your third finger?
-Are you using proper thumb placement on the back of the neck to allow the thumb to apply the most pressure?
-Are you squeezing hard enough?
-Are you strumming the 5th string by accident?

Rather than putting this chord in a progression at this point, my recommendation is once you form the chord and get each note to ring clearly without buzzing 🐝, take your fingers off the neck (leaving the thumb in place), and then reform the chord. Do this over and over to increase strength and accuracy.

Bb (four strings)

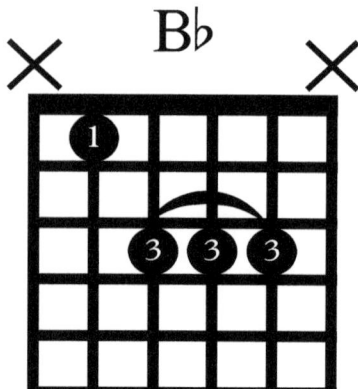

1. Place the first finger (somewhat flattened) on the first fret of the 5th string
2. Barre the third finger across the third fret of the 4th, 3rd, and 2nd strings (you do not need to angle backwards like you did with the first finger on the F chord)
3. Use the fleshy tip of your first finger to lightly mute the 6th string
4. Make sure to angle the third finger so that the 1st string is not sounding
5. Pluck each string from the 2nd to the 5th, one at a time to make sure all pitches sound
6. Remember to avoid the 1st and 6th strings in this chord

Troubleshooting the Bb chord:

-Is your third finger as straight across the third fret as you can make it?
-Are you still applying enough pressure to the first finger when the third finger comes in to play?
-Is your third finger barring too far so as to be sounding the note on the 1st string?
-Are you slightly touching the 6th string to mute the sound?

Try this progression to practice going in between the F (four strings) and Bb (four strings) chord shapes. Remember to focus on use the correct amount of strings in each chord, and only sound the pitches you need:

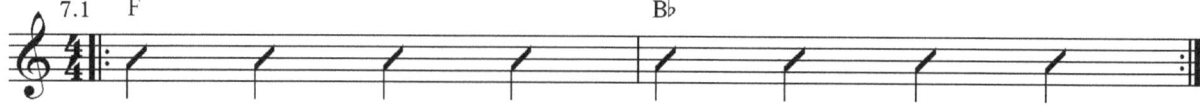

When that becomes comfortable, try switching faster:

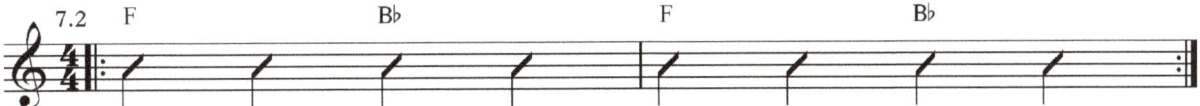

This exercise adds a familiar open chord to the progression:

Work out the upstrokes on this progression featuring solid 8th notes:

Try this one with a more complex strumming pattern:

Don't forget to use proper pick directions and tie the last 8th note into the first beat on the repeat.

The Movable Bb Chord

Much like the F chord, the Bb contains no open strings and is therefore a movable shape. It comes from the parent 👫 chord open A major. The first finger is again transposing the A chord to different keys and you move this shape up the fretboard. Try playing the Bb shape but starting your first finger on the third fret of the 5th string. You are now playing a C barre chord, which as you know, is a different voicing for the open C shape you have been playing thus far.

As mentioned in chapter 6, sometimes the ease of movability would be a factor in which voicing (open or movable) to use. Try progression 7.3 again, this time using a barre chord with a C shape (Bb moved two frets higher):

To get from the Bb to the C in this case, simply release the pressure on the strings and slide your shape up to the third fret, without adjusting your hand position. The same process applies in reverse when moving from the C back to Bb.

By not changing the finger shape you would in theory be able to execute this chord change much more smoothly. It also maintains a more consistent timbre by not having any open strings in the progression.

More detailed information about movable barre chord shapes will be provided in the coming chapters.

Individual vs. Simultaneous Fingerstyle Attack

In chapter 6 you learned the basics of fingerstyle guitar playing by performing rolling arpeggios. Very few examples contained attacks separated by string skips. As previously mentioned, one benefit of fingerstyle guitar technique is the ability to sound two notes simultaneously on non-adjacent strings. Although this can also be done with combination of the pick and fingers (a technique known as *hybrid picking*), it is more convenient to do this with the right hand unencumbered by the pick.

Try these exercises to strengthen simultaneous finger attack skills:

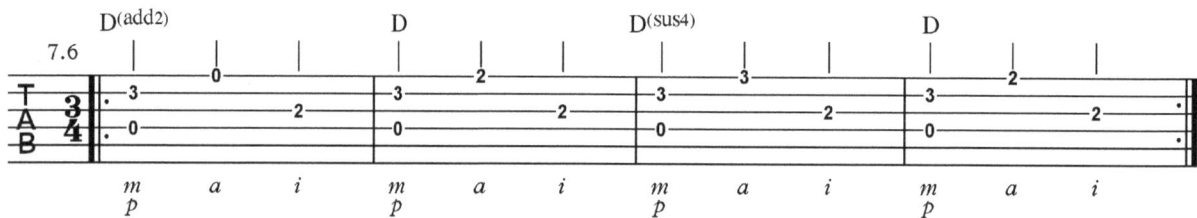

In exercise 7.7 your *i, m* and *a* fingers will stay on the 3rd, 2nd, and 1st strings respectively as you move your thumb (*p*) to follow the lowest note of each chord shape:

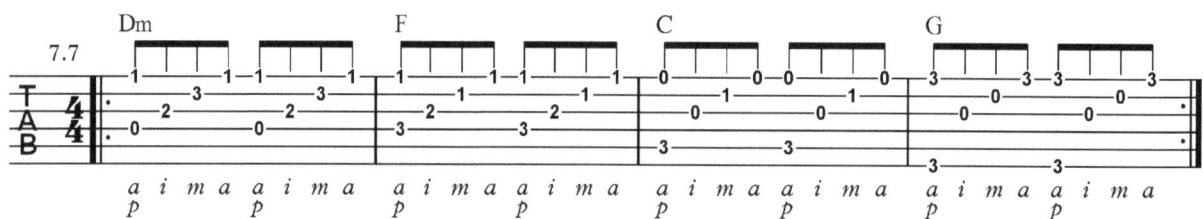

In exercise 7.8 your *i, m* and *a* fingers will stay on the 3rd, 2nd, and 1st strings respectively until the fourth measure containing the Bb chord. In that measure shift each finger over one string so that the *i, m* and *a* fingers land on the 4th, 3rd, and 2nd strings. Shift one string set higher as the progression repeats:

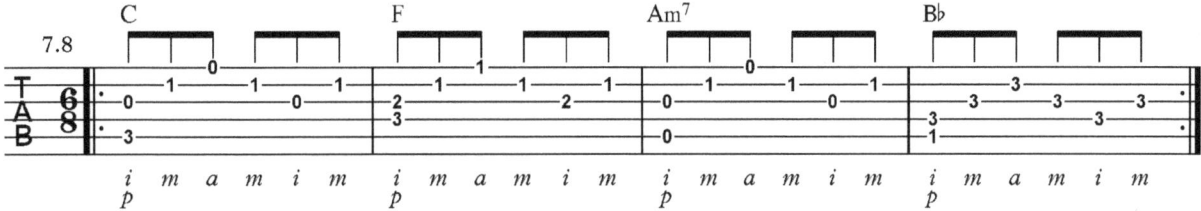

In exercise 7.9, practice jumping the thumb across string skips:

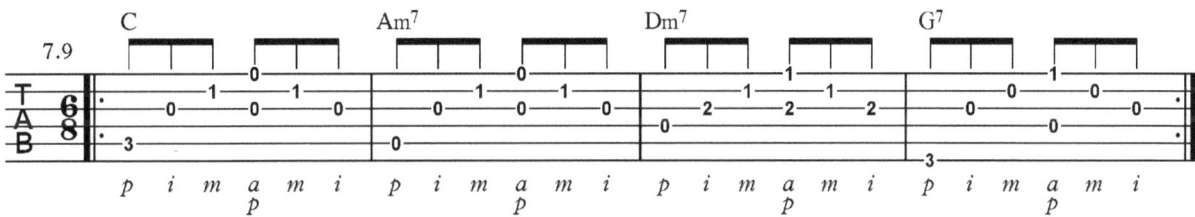

Example 7.10 will focus on using three fingers of the right hand simultaneously:

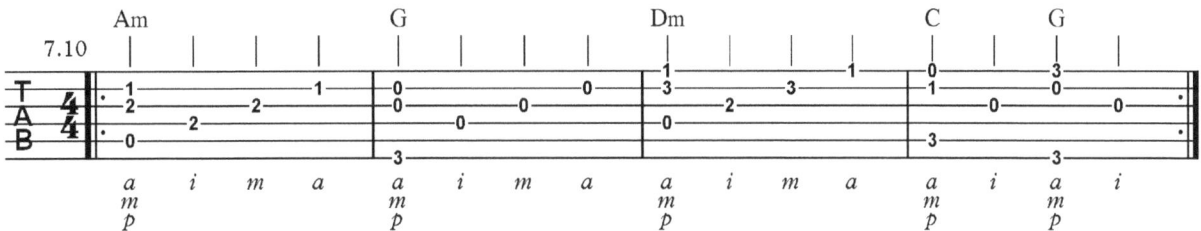

Important note: When playing fingerstyle guitar, it is not always necessary to form the entire chord shape if you do not pluck a given string within the chord. In the preceding example you would never need to use your second finger on either of the G chords or the C chord because that pitch is not being used. It will help you achieve faster switches to leave these fingers out. In the second measure you could also get away with only using the third finger to play the G, as the rest of the measure contains open strings. Keep an eye 👀 out for situations like this going forward.

Creating Right Hand Patterns

Perhaps the most rewarding experience in creating accompaniment patterns is realizing how many different variations you can achieve with the same basic pattern. Take for example this tried and true accompaniment pattern and the potential variants:

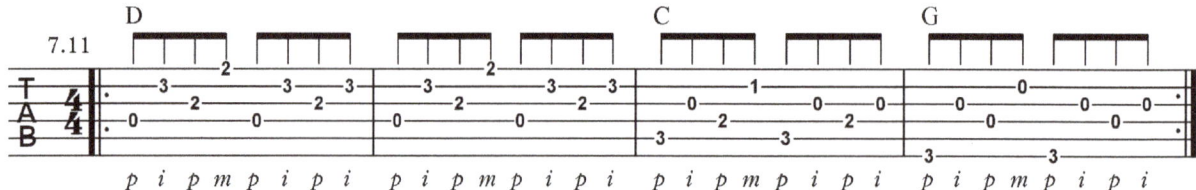

Here is a very systematic pattern that translates itself to the different string sets for the C and G chord. The next will be a variation that alternates the bass note similar to what we did with our pick in chapter 5:

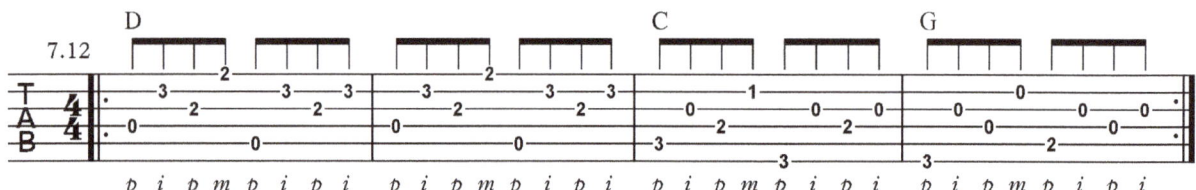

Notice on the G chord the bass note moves to the 5th string, rather than the 4th as we saw in Chapter 5. This is to avoid too much repetition to the open 4th string.

The next variation will employ simultaneous attacks to the pattern:

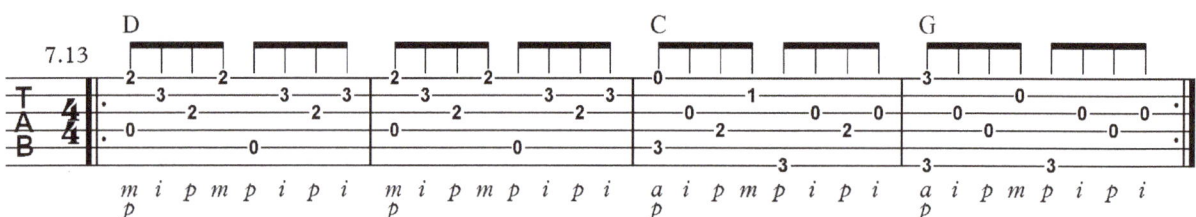

Take note here that the *m* and *p* fingers are used in conjunction on the closer split of the D chord, but the *a* and *m* fingers are used on the further splits of the C and D chords. Also in this example the bass note stays the same on the G chord, illustrating the concept that the pattern does not need to be identical throughout and may conform to make the right hand part more conducive.

Here is a variation to the rhythm:

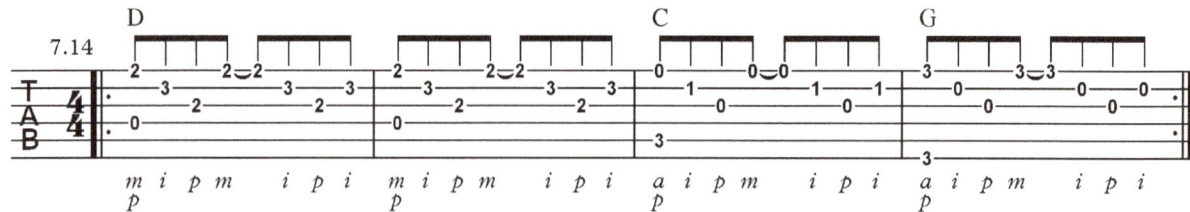

The "+" of beat 2 is tied into beat 3 to change the flow of the right hand. Also the string sets stays consistent throughout the chord changes save for the bass notes.

Here is the same rhythm with a different right-hand order:

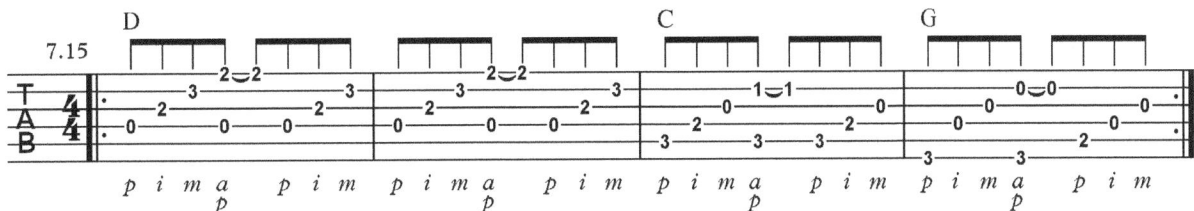

This time let's combine the previous two examples to make a two measure pattern instead of a one measure pattern:

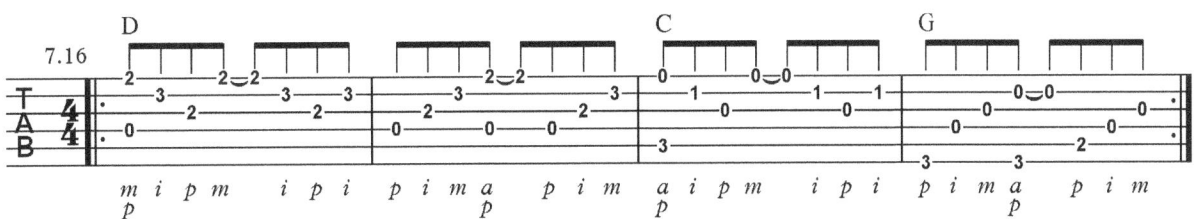

As you can see, there are numerous possibilities for creating fingerstyle accompaniment patterns. Here is a recap of some methods you could use to create your own:

1. Consistent right-hand pattern that adjusts strings to follow the chord shapes.
2. Consistent right-hand pattern that stays local to the strings only altering bass notes.
3. Pattern stays consistent as bass note alternates within each chord.
4. Steady pattern with simultaneous attack at the beginning of each measure.
5. Breaking the constant rhythmic flow with a held or tied rhythm.
6. Using a two measure repeated pattern instead of a one measure repeated idea.
7. Letting the chords decide the right-hand fingering.

Here is an example of the last idea:

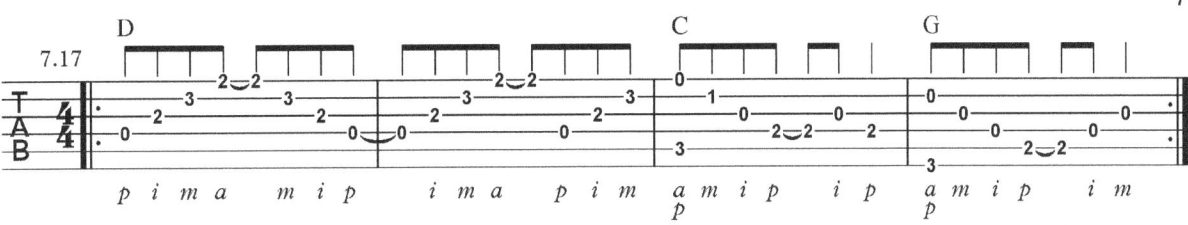

This pattern was created by just letting my right-hand fingering flow in its most natural motion. Not only did this process dictate the direction of the arpeggio, but also the rhythmic aspects.

Lastly remember that there is no substitute for experimentation and listening. You are only finished with your accompaniment pattern when your ear is content 🥰.

Chapter 7 Practice Progressions:

Create accompaniment patterns for the following progressions using one of the seven methods mentioned on the previous page (make sure to include right hand fingerings):

Chapter 8: Full Barre Chords and Power Chords

The time has come. There's no putting it off any further. We must now learn (🎼 Dun Dun Dunnnnn 🎵) FULL BARRE CHORD SHAPES 💀👻🤡😱😱😱. But do not fear! We have been working up to this moment by learning partial barre chord shapes. The strategies we used to the smaller shapes will also apply to the larger shapes.

Step 1: Finger Placement

As mentioned previously, when barring with your first finger you need to angle backwards to achieve the maximum use of your bone and achieve the straightest use of your finger.

Step 2: Strength Development

At first, having the strength to barre across all 6 strings seems impossible, especially if you are learning on a steel string acoustic guitar. But with proper strength training 🏆 in time you will be able to achieve this feat.

Strength training exercise:

-Barre the first finger across all six strings on the fifth fret
-Lean your finger backwards slightly towards the nut
-Press down as hard as you can, using the thumb to squeeze the neck
-Pluck each string to make sure it sounds

If you encounter any muted notes remember that 2 adjustments can go a long way.
1. Examine if any strings are falling into the grooves of your fingers and if so adjust the angle.
2. PRESS HARDER!!! Use anything that motivates you. Think of things you hate: traffic, paying taxes, politicians, student loans, etc.

Once you can get all strings sounding, remove your finger and try again. Keep up this routine until you can get all strings sounding on your first attempt, each time, five times in a row. Once you accomplish this, try the same exercise on the fourth fret. Continue to move one fret lower until you are able to achieve the first fret full barre.

*You may feel some pain 😵 in your thumb. This is normal, but remember to take breaks along the way. Eventually you will develop enough strength that you will not have to work so hard to get the sound. Keep this in mind as you develop because a lot of times the tendency is to over squeeze, which could cause pain and problems in the future. Most likely, however, that will not be the case for several months.

When you feel comfortable with your finger placement and strength, try to form the full F barre chord:

F:

1. Barre the first finger across the first fret of ALL six strings
2. Make sure all strings sound before proceeding further
3. Place the third finger on the third fret of the 5th string
4. Place the fourth finger behind it on the third fret of the 4th string
5. Place the second finger behind it on the second fret of the 3rd string
6. Pluck each string from the 6th to the first one at a time to make sure all pitches sound
7. Press down with the strength of 1,000 suns! ☀ x 1,000= F

Troubleshooting the F chord:

-Is your first finger angled backwards so as to be pressing on the flattest surface?
-Is the angle of your first finger shifting in the wrong direction when you add your other fingers?
-Are any of the established angles being compromised when you add your other fingers?
-Are you using proper thumb placement on the back of the neck to allow the thumb to apply the most pressure?
-Are you squeezing hard enough?

Rather than putting this chord in a progression at this point, my recommendation is once you form the chord and get it sounding clearly, take your fingers off the neck (leaving the thumb in place), and then reform the chord. Do this over and over to increase strength and accuracy.

Bb:

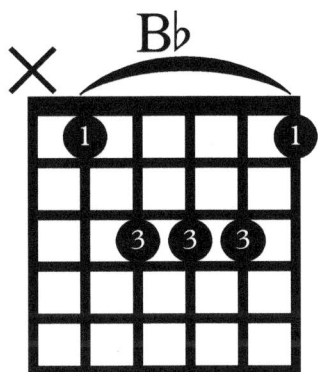

1. Barre the first finger across the 5th through 1st strings
2. Barre the third finger across the third fret of the 4th, 3rd, and 2nd strings angling it up so as to avoid making contact with the 1st string
3. Use the fleshy tip of your first finger to lightly mute the 6th string
4. Pluck each string from the 5th to the 1st, one at a time to make sure all pitches sound
5. Remember to avoid the 6th string in this chord

Troubleshooting the Bb chord:

-Is your third finger as straight across the third fret as you can make it?
-Are you still applying enough pressure to the first finger when the third finger comes in to play?
-Is your third finger barring too far so as to be sounding the note on the 1st string?
-Is the third finger bending up enough at the end to make sure the note on the 1st string is sounding?
-Are you slightly touching the 6th string to mute the sound?

> *The most challenging task you have faced this far is getting the third finger to bend upwards while still maintaining enough pressure to barre the necessary frets. Try practicing without the first finger in place before adding it in. Make sure the open 1st string rings as the rest is barred. When you can do that, try adding in the first finger.*

Try this progression to practice going in between the F and Bb chord shapes. From this point on we will **ONLY** be using the full voicings for these chords. Remember to focus on the correct pitch sequence in each chord, and make sure all notes ring clearly:

Transitioning from the 6th string to 5th string Barre Chord

It is extremely important to just roll your barre chord shape over when transitioning from the F to the Bb. This means the first finger should be set so that it barely moves from its position, lifting slightly so as to mute the 6th string. The third finger will edge over and flatten out. Remove the second and fourth fingers, but keep them close by so that they may return to position when switching back to the F shape.

When that becomes comfortable, try switching faster:

This exercise adds 1/8 note strumming to the progression:

Switch even faster!

Try adding a fingerstyle pattern:

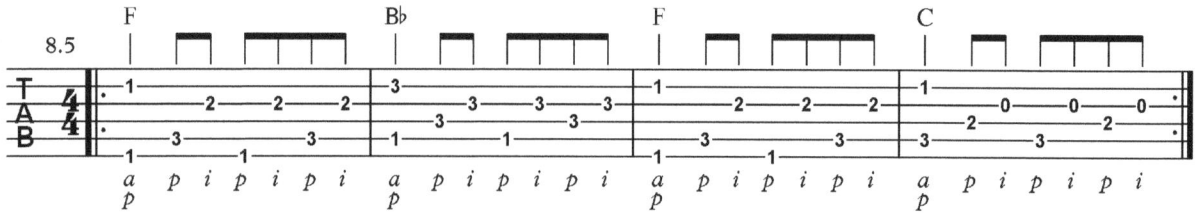

If you leave your first finger barred across all 6 strings on the Bb you can alternate your bass notes downward in the pattern:

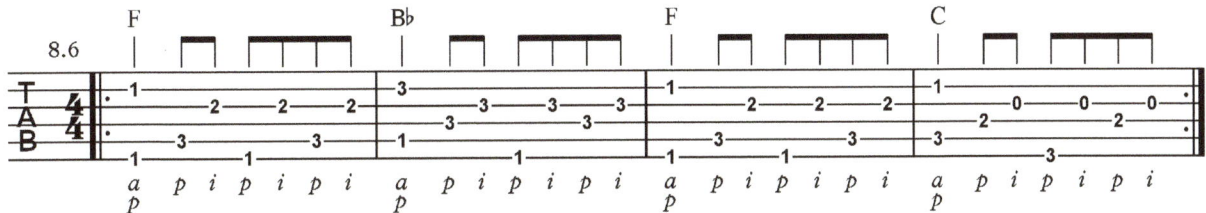

Work out the rhythms in the next two progressions:

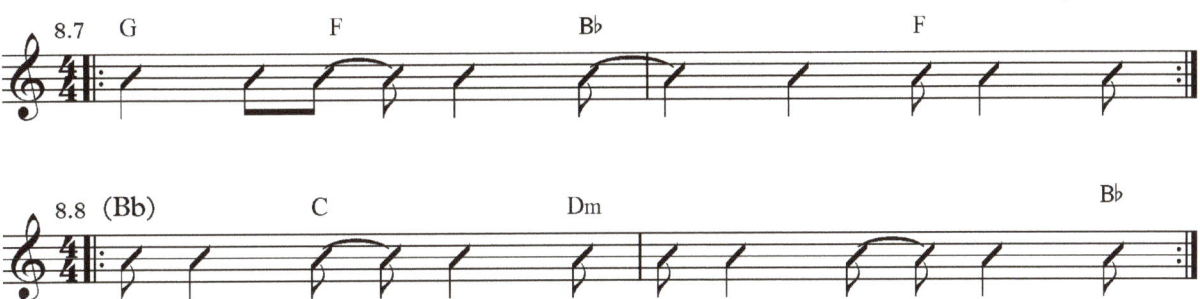

Don't forget to use proper pick direction. Watch the ties !

Modifiable Barre Chords

One convenient aspect of the two major barre chord shapes you have just learned, is the relative ease in which they can be modified into other chord qualities, such as minor and dominant 7. On the coming pages we will take our existing barre chord shapes, and with some slight re-fingerings, create two fundamental harmonic sounds.

Fm:

1. Barre the first finger across the first fret of ALL six strings
2. Make sure all strings sound before proceeding further
3. Place the third finger on the third fret of the 5th string
4. Place the fourth finger behind it on the third fret of the 4th string
5. Pluck each string from the 6th to the 1st, one at a time to make sure all pitches sound

Or:

1. Play and F chord
2. Remove the second finger
3. Pluck each string from the 6th to the 1st, one at a time to make sure all pitches sound

Troubleshooting the Fm chord:

-Is your first finger angled backwards so as to be pressing on the flattest surface?
-Is the angle of your first finger shifting in the wrong direction when you add your other fingers?
-Are any of the established angles being compromised when you add your other fingers?
-Are you using proper thumb placement on the back of the neck to allow the thumb to apply the most pressure?
-Are you squeezing hard enough?
-Double check the pitch on the 3rd string, this is the hardest one to get but is also the ONLY pitch making this a minor chord.

F7:

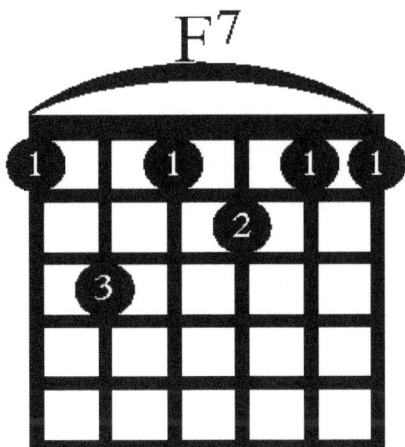

1. Barre the first finger across the first fret of ALL six strings
2. Make sure all strings sound before proceeding further
3. Place the third finger on the third fret of the 5th string
4. Place the second finger on the second fret of the 3rd string
5. Pluck each string from the 6th to the 1st, one at a time to make sure all pitches sound

Or:

1. Play and F chord
2. Remove the fourth finger
3. Pluck each string from the 6th to the 1st, one at a time to make sure all pitches sound

Troubleshooting the F7 chord:

-Is your first finger angled backwards so as to be pressing on the flattest surface?
-Is the angle of your first finger shifting in the wrong direction when you add your other fingers?
-Are any of the established angles being compromised when you add your other fingers?
-Are you using proper thumb placement on the back of the neck to allow the thumb to apply the most pressure?
-Are you squeezing hard enough?
-Double check the pitch on the fourth string, this is the hardest one to get but is also the ONLY pitch making this a 7th chord.

Bbm:

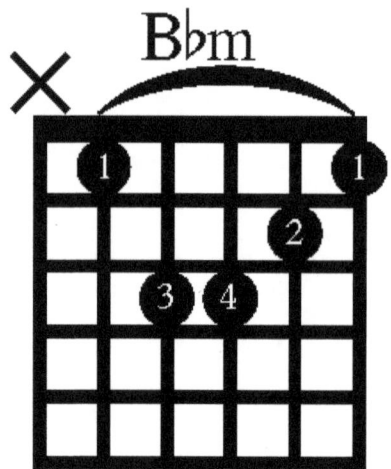

1. Barre the first finger across the 5th through 1st strings
2. Place the third finger on the third fret of the 4th string
3. Place the fourth finger behind it on the third fret of the 3rd string
4. Place the second finger behind it on the second fret of the 2nd string
5. Remember to avoid the 6th string in this chord

Or:

1. Play and F chord
2. Move every finger one string over (away from you)
3. Play each string from the 5th to 1st
4. Remember to avoid the 6th string in this chord

Troubleshooting the Bb chord:

-Is your first finger angled backwards so as to be pressing on the flattest surface?
-Is the angle of your first finger shifting in the wrong direction when you add your other fingers?
-Are any of the established angles being compromised when you add your other fingers?
-Are you using proper thumb placement on the back of the neck to allow the thumb to apply the most pressure?
-Are you squeezing hard enough?
-Are you slightly touching the 6th string to mute the sound?

Bb7:

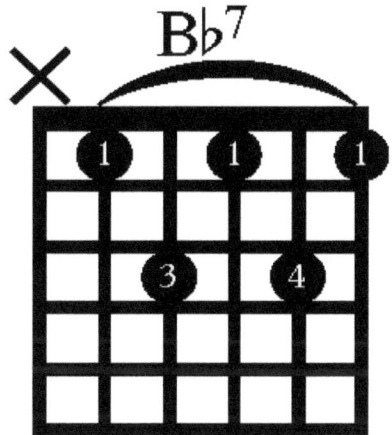

1. Barre the first finger across the 5th through 1st strings
2. Place the third finger on the third fret of the 4th string
3. Place the fourth finger on the third fret of the 2nd string
4. Use the fleshy tip of your first finger to lightly mute the 6th string
5. Pluck each string from the 5th to the 1st one at a time to make sure all pitches sound
6. Remember to avoid the 6th string in this chord

Troubleshooting the Bb7 chord:

-Are you still applying enough pressure to the first finger when the third and fourth fingers come in to play?
-Is your third finger accidentally muting the note on the 3rd string?
-Is your fourth finger accidentally muting the note on the 1st string?
-Are you slightly touching the 6th string to mute the sound?
-Double check the pitch on the third string, this is the hardest one to get but is also the ONLY pitch making this a 7th chord.

As always, practice bouncing back and forth between the chord shapes:

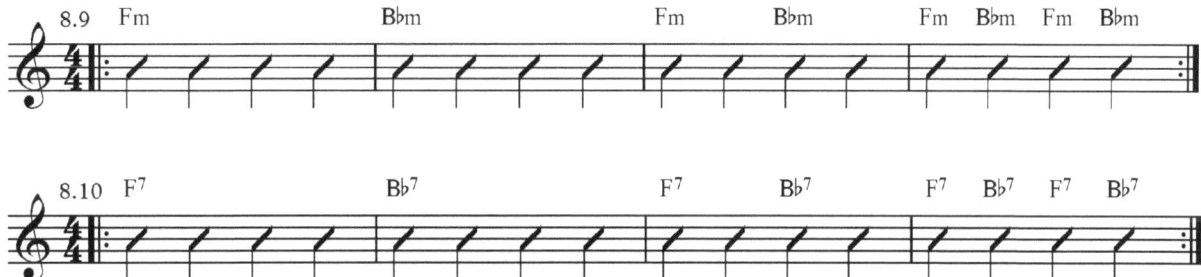

Power (5) Chords:

Power (5) chords are small chord shapes that focus on the lowest notes of the barre chord. These types of chords do not define major, minor or dominant sounds as they feature just a root and fifth (with the root being double up an octave). This type of chord is commonly used in rock music 🤘 as it creates a heavier sounding intervallic series.

Like the other chords you have learned, power (5) chords come in open and movable varieties:

E5:

1. Barre the first finger across the second fret of the 5th and 4th strings
2. Mute the 3rd and 2nd strings by angling the first finger slightly upwards at the end of the barre
3. Pluck each string from the 6th to the 4th to make sure all the pitches sound

There will be an added element of pick control here as you should avoid picking anything on the 1st string. It would be too difficult to mute all the remaining strings with your first finger. Make sure to focus your pick on the 6th, 5th, and 4th strings. If you make any incidental contact with the 3rd string it should be fine so long as you mute. Focus on strumming with wrist motion rather than elbow.

Troubleshooting the E5 chord:

-Is your first finger angled so as to mute the 3rd and 2nd strings?
-Are you hearing any higher notes when you strum this chord aggressively?

A5:

1. Barre the first finger across the second fret of the 4th and 3rd strings
2. Mute the 2nd and 1st strings by angling the first finger slightly upwards at the end of the barre
3. Pluck each string from the 5th to the 3rd to make sure all the pitches sound
4. Make sure to avoid the 6th string in this chord

The difficulty with the A5 chord is having the pick control to avoid the 6th string. Practice your right hand accuracy and use your wrist to strum from a fixed point.

Troubleshooting the A5 chord:

-Is your first finger angled so as to mute the 2nd and 1st strings?
-Are you hearing any of the 6th string when you strum this chord aggressively?

Bounce 🏀 back and forth between the two power (5) chords:

Practice with 8th notes to work on muting the higher strings and avoiding the 6th string on the A5 chord:

Movable Power (5) Chords

F5:

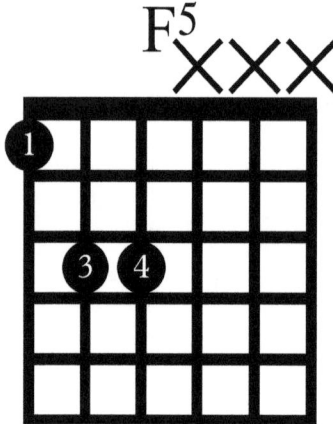

1. Lay the first finger across the first fret of all 6 strings pressing down ONLY on the 6th string, but muting the 3rd and 2nd strings
2. Place the third finger behind it on the third fret of the 5th string
3. Place the fourth finger behind it on the third fret of the 4th string
4. Pluck each string from the 6th to the 4th to make sure all the pitches sound

This chord is a movable version of the E5 chord. Any right hand techniques applied to the E5 should apply here as well.

Troubleshooting the F5 chord:

-Is your first finger angled so as to mute the 3rd and 2nd strings?
-Are you pressing down hard enough with the first finger on the 6th string?
-Are you hearing any higher notes when you strum this chord aggressively?

Bb5:

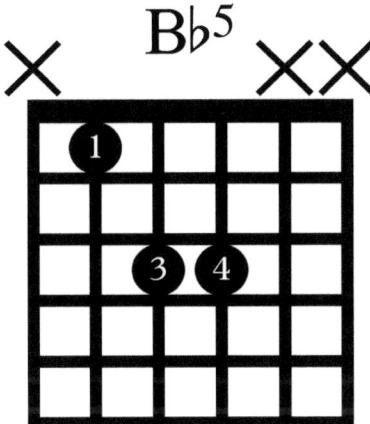

1. Lay the first finger across the first fret of the 5th through 1st strings pressing down ONLY on the 5th string, but muting the 2nd and 1st strings
2. Using the fleshy tip of your first finger, lightly touch against the 6th string to avoid it from ringing.
3. Place the third finger on the third fret of the 4th string
4. Place the fourth finger behind it on the third fret of the 3rd string
5. Pluck each string from the 5th to the 3rd to make sure all the pitches sound
6. Remember to avoid the 6th string in this chord

This chord is a movable version of the A5 chord. Any right hand techniques applied to the A5 should apply here as well.

Troubleshooting the Bb5 chord:

-Is your first finger angled so as to mute the 2nd and 1st strings?
-Are you pressing down hard enough with the first finger on the 5th string?
-Are you hearing any of the 6th string when you strum this chord aggressively?

*You may notice some guitar players fingering the movable power chord shapes by barring their third finger rather than using the third and fourth fingers. This is acceptable as well and may help with certain moves. It is also common to remove the highest octave (played by the fourth finger in our diagrams) to simplify the chord density and to make the shapes even easier to move. This will make more sense in the last two chapters as we explore further into movable shapes.

Try these power chord practice exercises:

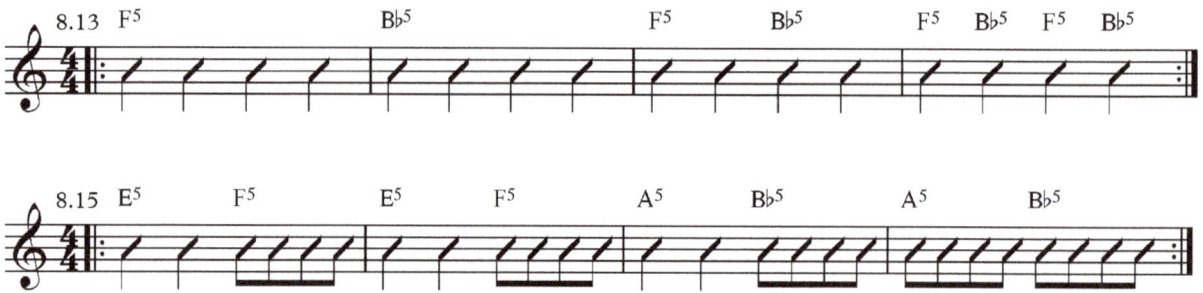

Metal bro 🎸🎵🎶

Chapter 8 Practice Progressions:

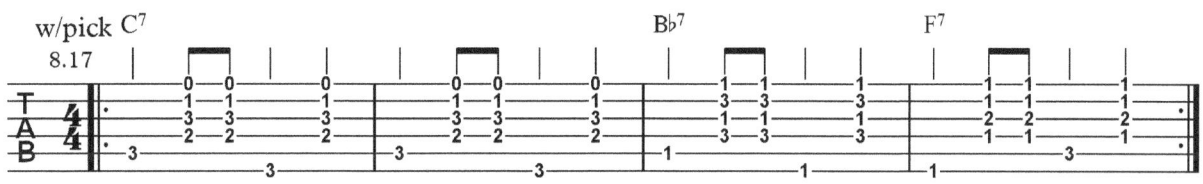

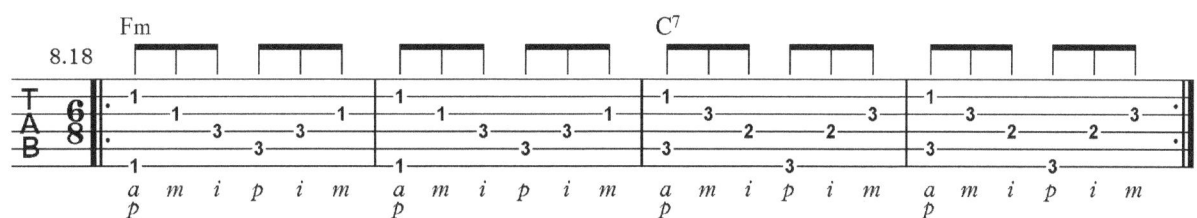

Chapter 9: Roots on the 6th String and Palm Muting

By now you have learned power chords and barre chords with the caveat that they are all movable shapes. It is time to learn how to figure out how to use the 6th string as a guide for finding chord names.

Look at the F major, minor, 7th and 5 chord shapes. Notice anything similar? Of course you did! You're an observant person 🧐. The placement of the notes on the 6th and 5th strings are identical in all four chord shapes. Ignoring the note on the 5th string (for now) we will focus on the lowest note of the chord on the 6th string, which is known as the **root** of the chord.

The F chord family is called "F"'s because the name of the note on the first fret of the 6th string is "F". 400 years ago in chapter 1 of this book you learned that the open 6th string is called "E". That's why the E major, minor, 7th and 5 chords start with the open E in the bottom.

One of the most important things to master on the guitar is quick recognition of the note names on the 6th string. Let's start by learning the natural note names using this impressive 😋 diagram:

Natural Note Names on the 6th String

Fret	Note
0	E
1	F
3	G
5	A
7	B
8	C
10	D
12	E
13	F
15	G

It is recommended that you use the dots on the side of the guitar to help visualize which fret is which. Take note of how the double dots on the twelfth fret conceptually start the neck over. The open string to the twelfth fret is a octave. The first fret to the thirteenth fret is also an octave, as is the third to the fifteenth and so on. This concept applies to any string on the guitar.

Memorizing Note Names

Begin by playing the open E on the 6th string. Using the impressive 😮 diagram play each individual natural note up to the fifteenth fret, saying each note name aloud. Repeat the process in descending order. Do this a few times with the diagram and then try without looking at it. Visualize how the dots help you align the fret and note name. Try having a friend quiz you in a random order. If you don't have a friend you may have some problems that this book cannot help you solve, but at least you have guitar!

When you feel comfortable with all of the natural note names, it's time to fill in the blanks:

Note Names on the 6th String

Nut	0	E
	1	F
	2	F#/Gb
	3	G
	4	G#/Ab
	5	A
	6	A#/Bb
	7	B
	8	C
	9	C#/Db
	10	D
	11	D#/Eb
	12	E
	13	F
	14	F#/Gb
	15	G

In between every fret that was left blank previously, you now see a **sharp** (#) or **flat** (b) sign. The way to understand this is simple: A sharp raises the pitch by a half step and a flat lowers a pitch by a half step. Remember it this way: if you sat on a *sharp* object such as a porcupine 🦔 you would jump up 😳. If your car 🚗 gets a FLAT tire it would lower 😞.

Repeat the exercise of ascending each individual note and saying the note names aloud, this time including the sharps or flats, a.k.a. **accidentals** 🤫. On the way up the neck, call each pitch by its sharp (#) name. On the way down call each pitch by its flat(b) name instead. When a pitch has two different names it is known as an **enharmonic**. As before use the diagram at first and when you feel comfortable take the diagram away.

The forgotten notes:

You don't see an E#/Fb or a B#/Cb on the diagram. That is because these pitches are enharmonic to natural note sounds. E#/Fb is the same sound as F, and B#/Cb is the same as B. These pitches do exist in theory, but for now it will be much easier to think of them by their natural names.

Cycle of 4ths and Circle of 5ths

Now that you have some familiarity with the note names on the 6th string, it is time to reinforce the concept. Unfortunately, just doing the ascending and descending exercises will not be enough to really help you visualize the notes names when needing to see them out of order. After all your brain is probably just cycling 🚴 through the letters of the alphabet to an extent. In order to really know where the note names on the string are, it's better to run through exercises that make you jump around. You can either get your friend to randomly call out note names, but a more self- reliant method is to use the cycle of 4ths/circle of 5ths method.

What is the cycle of 4ths/circle of 5ths?:

Since this is not a theory textbook (THANK GOD RIGHT!!??), I will give you a short answer to your fictionally presumed question. The 4th or 5th interval refers to that many pitches UP ⬆️ a major scale. In the key of C major (C D E F G A B C), F would be a 4th away from C and G would be a 5th away from C. In the cycle or circle however, each distance is *dependent* on the key. In the key of F the fourth higher would be a Bb, since Bb is contained within the **key signature**. The actual construction of the cycle and circle is not required for our purposes here. Our goal is to use these patterns to learn the note names of an individual string by having to jump wide distances.

Cycle of 4ths

C F Bb Eb Ab Db Gb B E A D G

We will use the cycle of 4ths to memorize our flats. If you ever do pick up that theory book you will learn how the cycle of fourths is very important to the flat key signatures. For now just use it to cycle through the notes on the 6th string, saying the notes out loud. Continually repeat through the cycle and try to increase your speed. The faster you can recognize the notes, the easier it will be for you to put chord progressions together. *Keep everything within the first twelve frets.* When you learn these, it should be pretty easy to see the note names above the twelfth fret.

Circle of 5ths

C G D A E B F# C# G# D# A# F

Use the circle of 5ths to memorize the note names as sharps. There is no priority when it comes to learning the note names as sharps vs. flats. Both are equally important and I would suggest spending the same amount of time on both. Try running through the note names of the 6th string with the cycle of 4ths and immediately follow up with the circle of 5ths. Do this enough times until you can recognize every single note on the 6th string in a timely manner.

The cycle of 4ths and circle of 5ths are actually mirror images of each other. Try reading the circle of 5ths backwards changing to the enharmonic flat of each pitch. Cool 😎.

Transposing Barre Chords

With the knowledge of where each root lies on the 6th string, you can now play a major, minor, 7th, and 5 (power) chord in every key simply by placing the first finger on the root and forming the chord shape behind it. Try these exercises with chord diagrams to help:

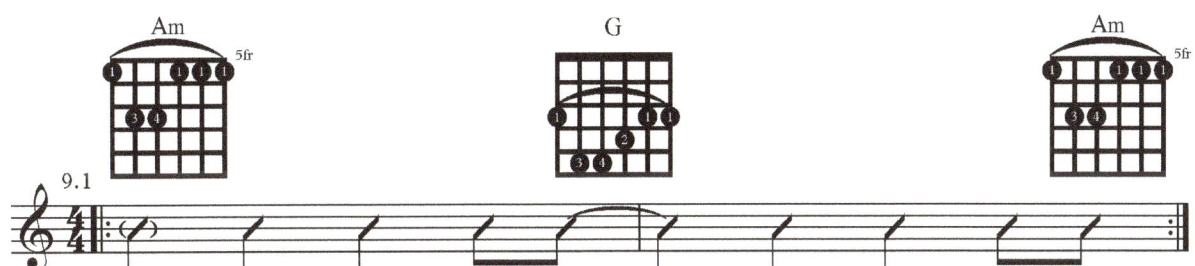

In the example above, the "5 fr" marking next to the Am chord indicates that the chord will lay out as follows starting from the fifth fret. This means the first finger will barre across the 5th fret and the third and fourth fingers will both be placed on the seventh fret of the 5th and 4th strings respectively. The G chord is shown as it would be played equivalent to the chord diagrams we have seen thus far. The barre sets up on the third fret. The parenthesis around the first strum indicates that this strum will only happen the first time through. On the repeat you will hold the tie from the + of 4 (Am).

Try some barre chords higher up the neck:

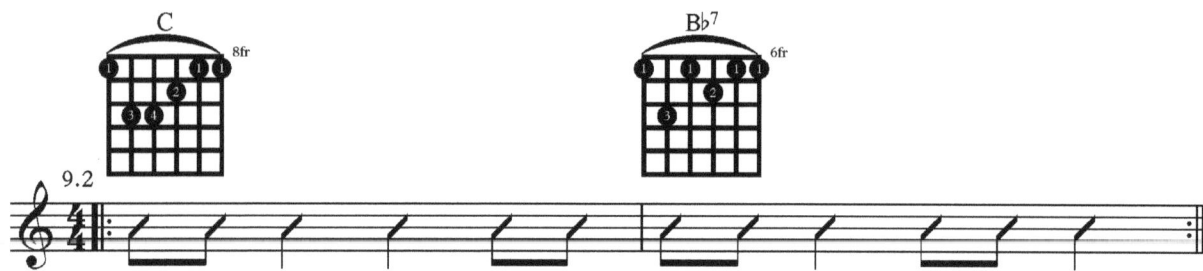

In this example we are playing two chords that we have learned previously in other areas of the neck. Try playing this same progression like this:

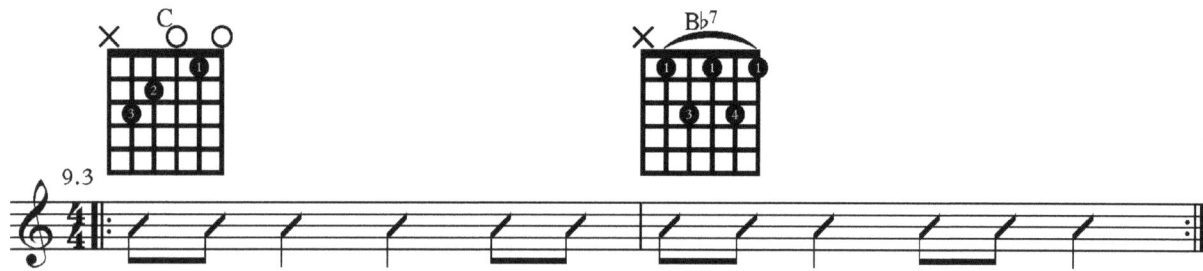

Play these two progressions and analyze the difference. You should notice a different in ease of playability, timbre, and chord density. Again, there are no wrong ways to put the chord sounds together, but use your songwriter's ear to decide which voicing order works best to fulfill your vision.

Try these next examples without the diagrams. Use **ONLY** barre chords on the 6th string:

148

Apply the concept to power chords:

Palm Muting Technique

Palm muting refers to the technique of dampening the resonance of the strings by applying slight pressure with your picking hand. Holding the pick between your index finger and thumb, extend you other fingers and place them on the bridge. Align the side of your hand to be completely straight against the bridge.

Palm Muting: Step 1

Now close up the hand.

Palm Muting: Step 2

Bring the pick downwards towards the strings without adjusting your palm's placement on the bridge.

Palm Muting: Step 3

Play this power chord progression (using an open E5) and slightly dampen the strings as you play. Don't overdo it!

The 'P.M.' follow by a dashed line indicates a palm mute. It also tells you how much of the part should be palm muted. Many parts might have palm muting of only specific areas.

Try this same progression as you add and remove the palm muting:

Be careful when you remove the palm mute to only lift your wrist as far as you need to have the strings ringing at their full capacity. Since the palm mute comes right back on the repeat you do not want to be too far away.

Palm Muting specifics:

The higher you move your right hand towards the neck will affect how muted the strings sound. Experiment moving the wrist slightly up and down the strings as you play. A small motion makes a big difference in terms of how much muting happens. If you move your hand too far towards the neck you could end up with no discernable pitch being produced. Just a series of thuds. While this could be used for a creative effect, you might want to focus on the harder aspect of palm muting, which is the more subtle muting sound.

Palm mutes tend to work best on power chords since you do not have to try to mute more than 3 strings at a time. But they can still be used effectively on larger chord shapes or even picked arpeggios!

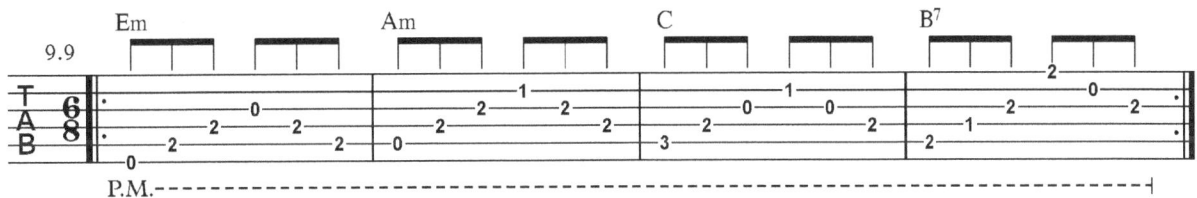

Palm muting is a great tool 🛠 for adding additional layers of texture to a guitar accompaniment. Experiment with some of your previously created progressions and see if palm muting can make it sound any better!

Chapter 9 Practice Progressions:

This time, the progressions are up to you because, after all, you are a songwriter! The most important thing is to try to heavily apply the chords and techniques learned in this chapter. But do not be afraid to use <u>anything</u> you have learned to far.

Here are a few things to think about that may inspire creativity:

1) Diatonic vs. Non-diatonic progressions: use your ear AND your brain 🧠
2) Open Chords vs. Barre Chords: it is playable? DO the voicings blend well together? Is there a better way?
3) Meter: 4/4? 3/4? 6/8? Something else?
4) Picking approach: Strummed? Arpeggiated (with pick or fingers)? Moving bass notes? Some combination of these?
5) Rhythm: 1/8 note based? 1/16th note based? Triplets? Ties? Syncopation?

You have worked on a ton of progressions and techniques in this book. But the most important aspect is for you to be able to take your knowledge and form your own ideas. Don't settle if you don't love something. Re-work it until you are proud of it.

I believe in you 👱.

Chapter 10: Roots on the 5th String and Offbeat Rhythms

When you are familiar with the names of the notes on the 6th string, it is time to learn the equally important 5th string:

Natural Note Names on the 5th String

Nut	0	A
	2	B
	3	C
	5	D
	7	E
	8	F
	10	G
	12	A
	14	B
	15	C

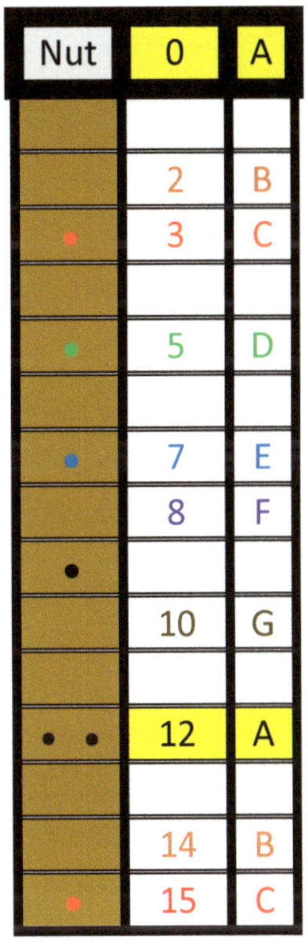

The 5th string lays out identical to the 6th string if you were to start from the 5th fret. You may remember that concept from learning to tune your guitar by ear in chapter one (6th string fifth fret = open 5th string). The challenge now is to not confuse yourself with the note arrangement of the 6th string. Start from scratch and memorize the natural note names on the 5th string. Ascend and descend the natural notes in order, saying the names aloud. Try to memorize it.

Note Names on the 5th String

Nut	Fret	Note
	0	A
	1	A#/Bb
	2	B
	3	C
	4	C#/Db
	5	D
	6	D#/Eb
	7	E
	8	F
	9	F#/Gb
	10	G
	11	G#/Ab
	12	A
	13	A#/Bb
	14	B
	15	C

No surprises here. Just a new string set to memorize. As you did with the 6th string, memorize the individual note names chromatically in order and then put them through the cycle of 4ths and circle of 5ths. Say the note names as you increase your speed.

Moveable Barre Chords with the 5th String Root

Think about your open A and Bb barre chord shapes. These are the chord shapes you should apply to the 5th string roots. Try some progressions with these shapes.

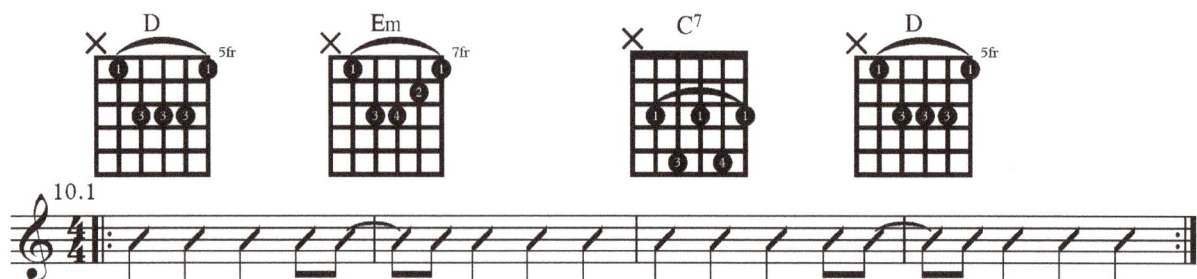

10.1

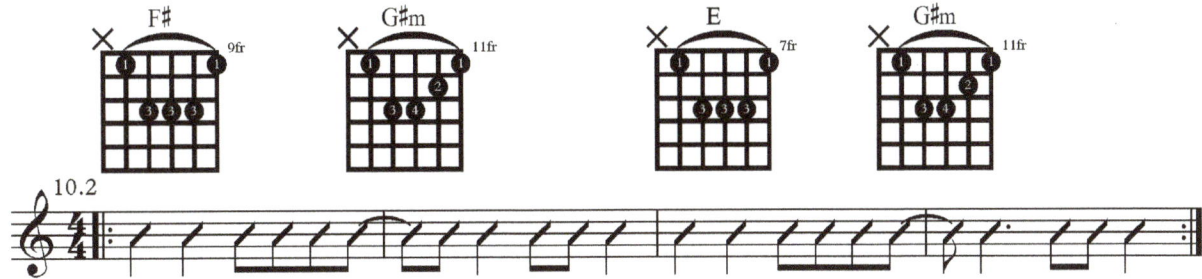

Learning to Combine the 6th and 5th string Moveable chords

The biggest reason to learn roots on the 6th and 5th strings are so you can move back and forth in between them. This will allow you to shorten the distance between chords of larger intervals jumps, such as 4ths and 5ths.

Note Names on the 6th and 5th String

Nut	0	E	A
	1	F	A#/Bb
	2	F#/Bb	B
	3	G	C
	4	G#/Ab	C#/Db
	5	A	D
	6	A#/Bb	D#/Eb
	7	B	E
	8	C	F
	9	C#/Db	F#/Gb
	10	D	G
	11	D#/Eb	G#/Ab
	12	E	A
	13	F	A#/Bb
	14	F#/Gb	B
	15	G	C

In this graph, the colors are coded so that they match the same note names. A great exercise is to take the cycle of 4ths and circle of 5ths and play through them again, this time bouncing from the pitch on the 6th string to the pitch on the 5th string. Some notes will be unison and others will be octaves. You only need to do this on the first 12 frets for now.

For example: C (eighth fret, 6th string/third fret, 5th string)

When you can do this with ease for all the pitches, proceed to doing it with chord shapes. Play your major, minor, 7th, and power chords starting on the 6th string and then quickly moving to the 5th string:

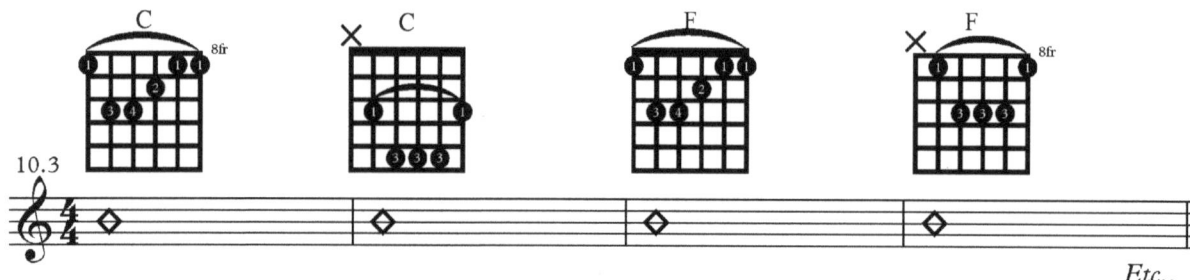

Etc..

Go through the cycle and circle this way with all the qualities. This should give you a really good idea where your options lie for any particular movable chord voicing.

Try these exercises to move between the barre chords on the 6th and 5th strings:

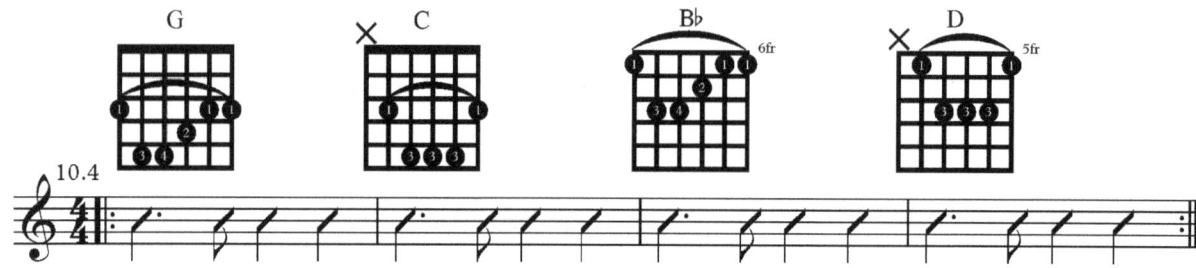

When moving directly across from the G to C chord, make sure to roll the fingers like we practice with the F-Bb barre chords in chapter 8. The same will apply from Bb to D with a shift down one fret.

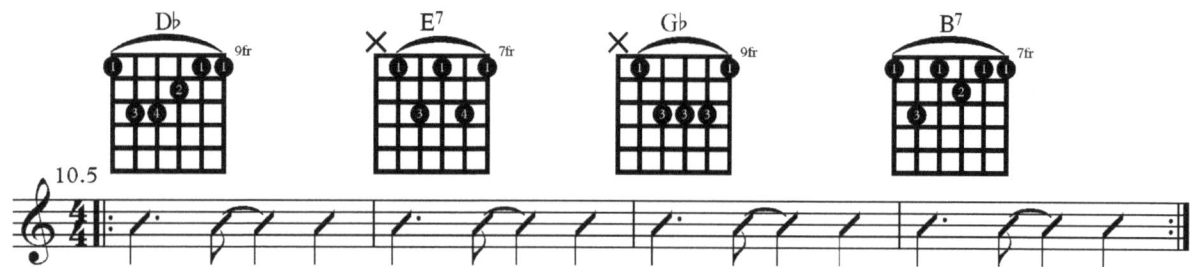

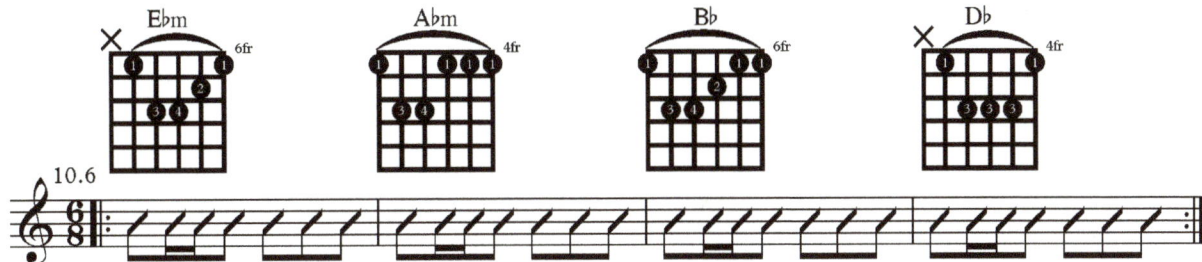

Connecting Progressions

The best way to arrange your movable progressions would be to find the <u>closest</u> path to connect all the chords. This would include consideration for when the chord progression repeats back to the beginning. Take for example the following progression:

The first decision to make is where you will begin. In this example we will forego the use of open chords and focus solely on barre chords.

OPTION A: Starting the progression on the 6th string.

Suppose you decide to start the progression with the C rooted on the 6th string. The most convenient way to play the chords would look like this:

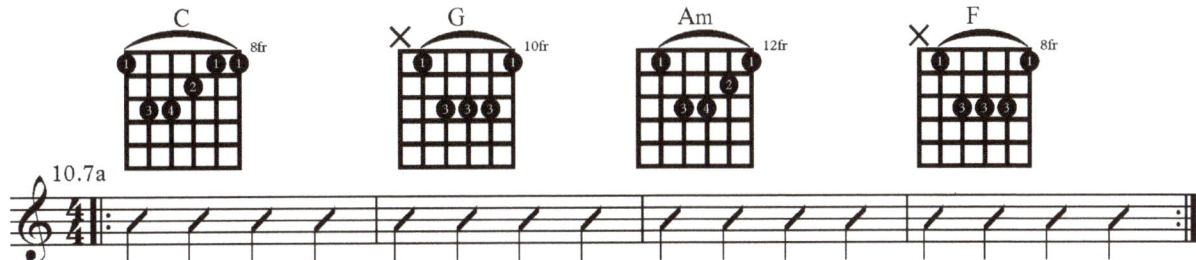

Notice how each chord is about two frets away from the next, with the exception being from the Am to F in the third and fourth measure. You might see that an F chord on the thirteenth fret would be closer to the Am **BUT** then the path from F to C would be even further. Now when we switch from F to C we need to simply move right across the strings on the eighth fret landing us right back where we started. This creates a nice box 📦 that is relatively easy to play and will sound consistent. If the chords jump too far away from each other it gets hard to execute physically and can also be hard for the ear to follow. From a songwriting standpoint this might also take up too much range in a mix if other instruments are involved.

OPTION B: Starting the progression on the 5th string.

Since you know a C major barre chord on the 5th string also, let us look at the optimal progression for starting there:

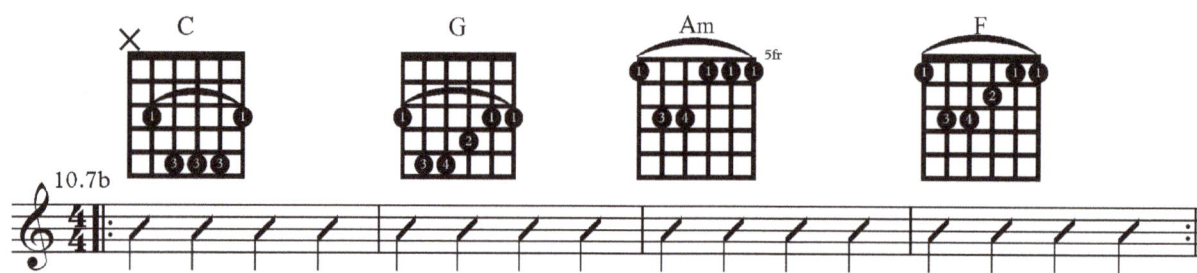

This is a very similar process in which the chords all switch to close positions with the farther switch from Am to F being executed to create a convenient path back to the start of the progression.

It is key 🔑 to be able to locate the closest versions of each barre chord in a progression. Every progression below should be conceived starting from the 6th string and then again starting from the 5th string:

Make sure to switch chords on the indicated beat.

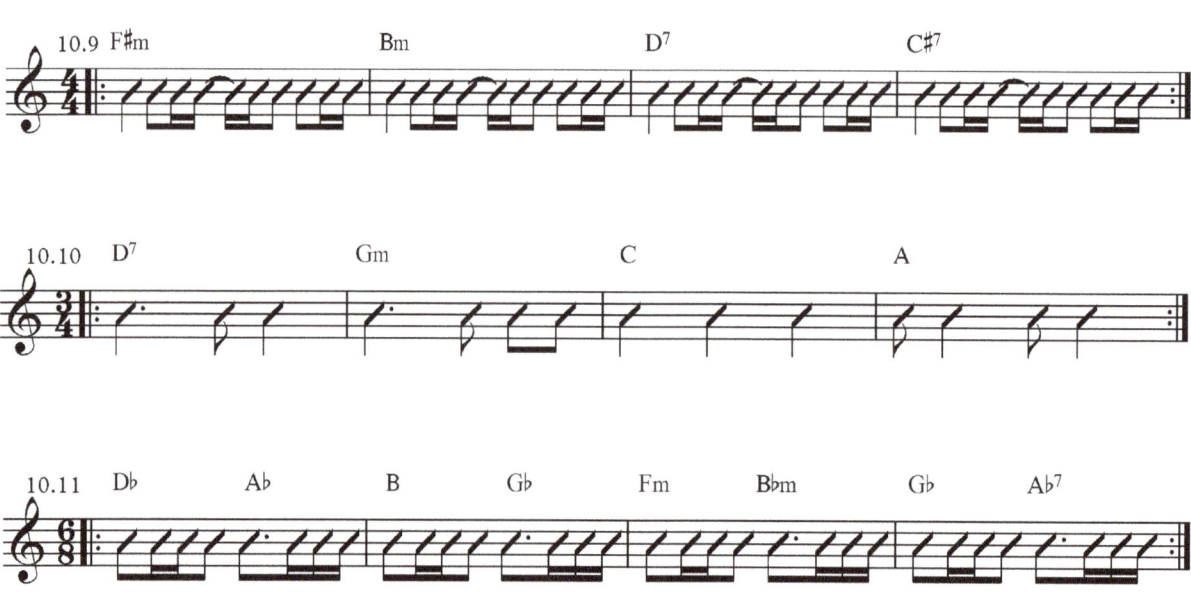

Executing Off Beat Rhythms

Some musical styles, such as reggae or ska, require consistent **staccato**, or short, off beat attacks. This would mean the attacks on the "+" of each beat. In between you would want to deaden the sustain of each chord to emphasize the initial pick strike. This is hard to accomplish with open chords as muting the open strings in the manner can be quite challenging. However, you can accomplish this quite easily with bar chords by simply lifting your left hand off the strings while holding the chord shape. This will not only silence the strings, but leave you in a position to replay the same chord when needed.

Try these examples. Focus on playing ONLY upstrokes with the right hand and making sure the sound does not carry from one chord strike to the next:

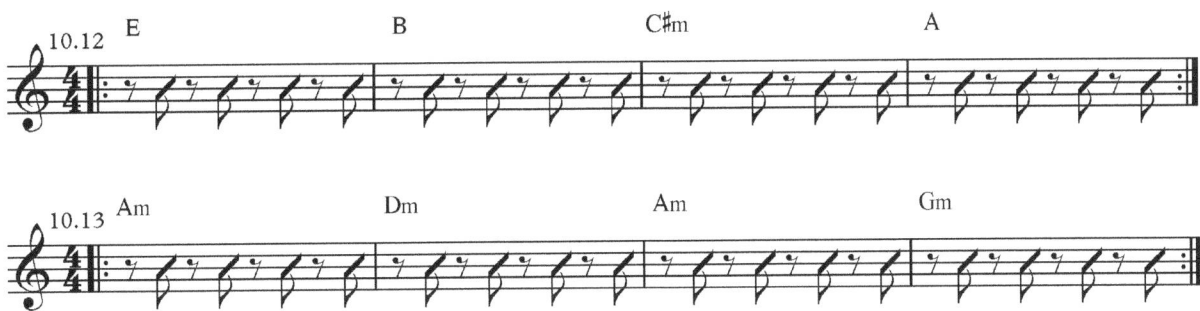

Check this common variation:

On all of these examples focus primarily on the higher 3 to 4 strings of the chord for the most authentic sound.

Conclusion: Now What?

I'm afraid you have reached the end of this book, but you have not reached the end of your guitar playing. The skills you have learned up to this point will get you started on writing Pop, Rock, Country and Reggae music. You should be able to create very traditional sounding rhythm guitar parts for these styles. And yet there is much more to learn....

The information given here will last you for quite a while and I recommend completely mastering everything before taking the next step in your journey. Mastering means the ability to play any chord progression in the book flawlessly and in tempo. You will have all the open chord shapes memorized as well as all the roots on the 6th and 5th strings. If you want to dive further into the world of guitar it would be wise 🧐 to seek out a private instructor.

Here are the next steps to take with a private instructor:

-more barre chord sounds: sus4, 7sus4, min7
-additional 7th chords: Maj7, min7b5, diminished 7
-augmented and diminished triads
-more in-depth right hand techniques
-scales and arpeggios
-and of course more rhythmic, technique, style, and songwriting concepts…

I thank you for taking the time to go through this book. I'd like to leave you with some final advice.

A songwriter must bend the rules. A songwriter must occasionally break the rules. SAY SOMETHING original with your music, whether it be through the lyrics or a unique accompaniment part or melody. Always be true to yourself and your vision. Edit and modify. A song has the power to immortalize your thoughts. This is a great honor to do this.

And lastly….

Enjoy the process!

About the Author

Ian Robbins graduated from USC with a Bachelor's and Master's degree in Studio/Jazz performance. He has had airplay on KJAZ 88.1FM and other national jazz stations as a member of the Bruce Escovitz Jazz Orchestra (BEJO). He recorded on BEJO's 2008 Album Invitation. Invitation spent several weeks in the top half of the Billboard Jazz charts. Ian recently recorded Guitar, Ukulele and Mandolin tracks for a song used for a promotional video for the NBC TV Show *This Is Us*. Lately Ian has performed with Landau Eugene Murphy Jr.- The winner of NBC's *America's Got Talent* Season 6. Ian has previously performed/recorded with Barry Manilow, Bonnie Raitt, Wynton Marsalis, Peter Erskine, Toni Tennille, Louis Bellson, Ndugu Chancellor, Stu Hamm, Kurt Elling, Ernie Watts, Marilyn McCoo, Alan Chang, Scott Henderson, and many others. Ian has also done session work for Grammy winning producer Bobby Watson and for Nickelodeon Studios. Recently Ian recorded for the JGAH project in Korea (arranged by Dr. Rachel Yoon), a Korean traditional music group that has performed live over 200 times along to Ian's prerecorded fusion guitar tracks.

Ian is currently on the faculty at Musician's Institute. As part of the Bachelor Degree Program he teaches Guitar Technique, Guitar Reading, Songwriting, Performance Classes in Punk, Blues Rock and Fusion (the latter with former co/teacher Russell Ferrante), Ear Training, Private Lessons and Open Counseling. He also teaches the KPOP, Zawinul and Coffee House International LPWs.

Ian Robbins is also the lead guitarist/singer/songwriter of original punk rock band Get Out™. Get Out™ has released 6 albums, which have sold on 6 continents and performed hundreds of shows. Get Out™'s YouTube channel currently has over 40,000 views (none of which were purchased). They have been endorsed by energy drink company Nitro 2 Go and have gotten airplay on various local stations. The band has performed on LA18 television and has shared the stage with such national acts as Voodoo Glow Skulls, Streetlight Manifesto, MXPX, and Suburban Legends. In January 2015, Get Out™ released *Epilogue* with the help of drummer Jeff Bowders (Paul Gilbert, Shakira). *Epilogue* is a 19 minute progressive punk rock epic currently being sold on iTunes and other online distributors. Get Out™ will release their 7th album *We Were Here First* this year.

Ian is a member of Hip Hop/Electronica group Dancing Mischief, which has received airplay on KCRW FM.

Ian also plays guitar for Korean Grammy winning artist Ann One. Ann One has performed at KCON 2018, the Korean Society of Maryland's annual festival, on LA18's Halo Halo, and was featured on the pilot episode of the Asian American web series *Sessions at Studio 5A*.

www.ingramcontent.com/pod-product-compliance
Lightning Source LLC
Chambersburg PA
CBHW041111070526
44584CB00002B/135